LEADERSHIP
IMPERATIVES
LIVING AND LEADING BEYOND 2020

Dexter John Valles

Copyright © Dexter John Valles, 2020

ALL RIGHTS RESERVED. No part of this book may be reproduced or transmitted in any form whatsoever, electronic or mechanical, including photocopying, recording, or by any informational storage or retrieval system without the express written, dated and signed permission from the author.

Author : Dexter John Valles
Title : Leadership Imperatives : Living & Leading Beyond 2020
Categories : Inspiration & Personal Growth, Success, Motivation, Leadership
Inspired by : The Holy Spirit

First Edition July 2020

DEDICATION

This book is my sixth this year and is dedicated to my ardent supporters and fans (I can get away with this here !)

***My beloved wife
Maria P Valles
&
My darling daughter
Valerie Anne Valles***

And in Honour of all those countless Leadership Lessons learned at home from the lives of my Beloved Parents
***Edmund Rudolf Valles &
late Clothilda Teresa Valles***

CONTENTS

INTRODUCTION

Part One : A Changed Landscape
Chapter One : The Landscape of Personal Life
Chapter Two : The Landscape of Education and Career
Chapter Three: The Landscape of Work Life

Part Two : New Scripts of Success
Chapter Four: Clarity of Now
Chapter Five: Competence for Tomorrow
Chapter Six: Commitment to Change

Part Three : The New Leadership Imperatives

Chapter Seven: The Warrior Leader: Business Crisis Centered Leadership:
Chapter Eight: The Digital Leader: Technology Centered Leadership
Chapter Nine: The EQ Savvy Leader: Heart Centered Leadership
Chapter Ten: The Ignited Leader: Spirit Centered Leadership

What Really Matters
A Leader's Legacy

AFTERWORD

INTRODUCTION

Thank you for buying and reading this book !

The landscape of the world has changed dramatically since Covid-19 hit our lives.

This is perhaps the most Metamorphic Transformation of the world we have ever witnessed in our lifetime. Stories shall be told about these days throughout history. We are part of those stories.

They are about how we stood up and were counted. How lives and livelihood were protected and promoted. How business design and strategy evolved to reshape and reframe the future. And how Leadership emerged from the darkness of the Lockdown to shine brightly in the sky.

Like the Sun. Burning away inequalities and inequities of the past, and growing a planet of people determined to survive, thrive and flourish, together !

LEADERSHIP IMPERATIVES

This book is about how that can happen. These are the pages which describe the making of the History of this New Earth !

Let's begin this book by taking a look at the elements of this landscape so that we can understand the change. Then move on to the Three New Scripts of Success and finally the Four New Leadership Imperatives.

As you read you will find that this book is not based on conventional straight-jacketed management wisdom. You may even find yourself challenged to look through the lens I am offering.

My purpose is to do exactly that. Through this book, I am offering another view, one emerging from my own experiences and emotions, of being prime witness to this churn, in managing the new normal, or as it is being called, the next normal of life beyond 2020

So, this is more of a Life Primer, of Leadership in Life and at Work. Nothing is as Imperative as you enabling yourself to lead the charge of life.

Put the wisdom from the pages which follow, along with your own and draw up a dynamic blueprint for yourself and those whose lives you influence.

LEADERSHIP IMPERATIVES

PART ONE

A CHANGED LANDSCAPE

THE DAWN OF A NEW EARTH

The real voyage of discovery consists not in seeking new landscapes, but in having new eyes

Marcel Proust

Part One
A Changed Landscape

Chapter One

The Landscape of Personal Life

Chapter Two

The Landscape of Education and Career

Chapter Three

The Landscape of Work Life

CHAPTER ONE
THE LANDSCAPE OF PERSONAL LIFE

What a dramatic shift !! Everything we chased with such intensity and speed has come to an almost dead halt. No pun intended ! Meaning of life we sought through our pre-pandemic pursuits have turned out to be shallow and hollow. Nothing matters more than surviving this Pause.

Dreams and Aspirations

In truth we have had the time to reflect and realize what is really important. Old dusty dreams and aspirations have been taken off the shelf, cleaned and reexamined. Perhaps partly because they may hold the key to survival in the future. It would be interesting if everyone did this. A whole new world would emerge. Sounds really exciting ! So much can change. We are change junkies and change makes our adrenaline flow.

It would help if we stop agitating about what we are losing and climb aboard the Change Bus. You see, our tickets have already been punched.

For me personally, as a learning facilitator in behavioural skills and a life coach, I have rediscovered my dream of being an author. Over 32 years I have crafted an interesting life. But it took me seventeen years of busyness with my life, to find the time and mental space to write and publish my first book "The Butterfly Blueprint" on Amazon in May 2020. Ever since, I have written four more and this is Number Six !!

Suddenly life is flowing with the full flush of vitality in the midst of being stuck. What an amazing contradiction! I wouldn't believe this could have happened if someone had tapped me on the shoulder and confided this to me.

Maybe you have a long-lost dream, or old forgotten, abandoned, skills stored away. No matter how insignificant they may seem to the canvass of life we were painting, like fine paint brushes, they can shape and add character to the large splashes on that canvas. This would be a good time to find our way back to them. I can assure you that you shall find release and flow!

Friendships and Relationships

Ever since the world locked down, I have reconnected with a host of friends. Even though some of us found time for each other earlier, today we actually know more about each other's lives and careers. It's amazing how close you can be and yet not truly know enough about people. And when we are torn apart, if we make the effort to stay connected, we shall find that we uncover and connect with parts others' lives, we were hardly aware of !

Discovering our dreams connects us to other people's dreams too. Living our dreams in such times of trouble is an inspiration to others struggling with staying afloat. When lives connect via our dreams, such connections quickly turn into new or better friendships and stronger relationships.

Such is the richness of life, we are rewarded with when we reach out to make our lives count.

Going forward into the new design of a future which is in clear sight, these friendships and relationships will thrive. Because they were forged in crisis. A friend in need is a friend indeed. Meaning has returned to this phrase.

Learning and Development

This has been changing steadily for the past several years. With IT bringing revolutionary change to how we learn. So much is available to everyone. Anybody with an internet connection or a smartphone can learn about almost anything.

The new normal which is in progress has already shown the way and opened doors to a Digital World. Information barriers have been pulled down to allow children to learn by exploring their world through digital devices. The flood of information has not yet been carefully curated and cultured into knowledge and application but I can see that we are getting there. The downside is that the attraction of the digital world is fatal. It takes prisoners never to be released. It spreads quicker than Cancer and yet, like permanent sunlight is everywhere all the time.

At the organizational level, the traditional learning & development classroom is likely to give way to the e-Classroom. Webinars, e-modules, interactive e-courses are easier to access and attend. Costs of travel and fixed learning times needing employees to leave their work places and duties to attend contact workshops is immediately saved. Access is wider since sessions are stored and can be offered to anyone at anytime !

It's not without its difficulties like getting people to work in groups, experience physical teamwork, use synchronous time interaction, share energy and bond are some advantages llkely to be lost. Though the design and delivery of such learning is already experiencing change to compensate this loss, and produce a whole new energy of learning.

Leadership which leverages this ahead of the curve will have created a vibrant and appealing learning space which can make every employee move rapidly to an enhanced level of capability and potential. A feeling of personal competence and value.

That's where growth lies.

CHAPTER TWO
THE LANDSCAPE OF EDUCATION AND CAREER

Redefining Education and Career

It's not just how education is changing. From college campuses to online communities of students. This is more about what the student is learning. The need to qualify for the traditional streams and subjects is experiencing a remarkable shift. We have to watch for total abandonment of some areas. Which will bring down the daunting entry barriers with a crash and invite participation from students truly interested in learning these professions. Like engineering, medicine, technology and several super specializations usually out of reach of several eligible candidates because of terrifying entry barriers. Education is evolving where both the student and the teacher form mutually accountable learning partnerships. It's the new way of life. The joy and energy of learning as committed communities must be tapped and delivered into the life of each individual student and teacher.

Reassessing Yourself

Take the time to reassess yourself. What's working for you now. What's not. What can work for you. Look at what the world is doing but do not be unduly influenced. Most of us are struggling to find our feet too.

There are many people reaching back into the past to yank what worked then into what is the Landscape of today. Sometimes disguised as new tools. Like the endless webinars loaded with learning and advice from lessons of the past and those imagined for the future. The present being discounted. But the present is the bridge to the future.

Without acknowledging the present moment in all its colourful chaos, you can't really reach the future. You need to take a step back to look, observe, reflect and reimagine what may be the future. Rushing headlong armed with bags fully loaded with sharpened tools of the past isn't the way forward.

Reassessing yourself is about looking at the evolving environment and how you can contribute to the new future. In a way that does not simply piggy back on what you did earlier, because that will follow you anyway. You must look at how you can leap across your own old ways, newly acquired disbeliefs and doubts. Stretch across chasms and risk your safety for unclear rewards.

Discovering the new earth unfolding before you, cannot be done by map reading. Of old maps which are already being redrawn in ways that make them unrecognizable. Because the Landscape we once knew, like the back of our hands, has truly changed !

Reevaluating Choices

Reassessing yourself, participating in redrawing maps of the future, risking your safety, reassessing yourself in this new world, opens the gates to choices and options. Reevaluating choices can only occur when you realize that you have them to begin with.

Today I have a choice of returning to being a corporate trainer and consultant or add being an author-speaker, where I generate my own content, of how I evaluate the world, with my insights, and share that with others. With increased emphasis as a life coach. That's one set of choices staring at me in the face. There may be other choices which shall emerge from there. I can piggy back on my old skills and add digital platforms to support the classroom learning process I usually deliver. It should work too. Amongst the hundreds of others doing the same thing, I can now redefine my offering with the newer aspects of my life. But is that enough, I wonder?

Just as I am at these crossroads, so are you. What would you embrace and do, as a sign of leading your life forward with new purpose and inspiring others too at the same time? What are you willing to risk and run with that risk before the growing risks of emerging life start chasing you?

CHAPTER THREE
THE LANDSCAPE OF WORK LIFE

The World Economic Crisis of 2020

The COVID-19 Pandemic has triggered the deepest global recession in decades. The pandemic is expected to plunge most countries into recession with economies contracting in the largest measure globally since the 19th Century, including advanced economies of the world.

According to the World Bank's June 2020 Global Economic Prospects Report "a particularly concerning aspect of the outlook is the humanitarian and economic toll the global recession will take on economies with extensive informal sectors that make up an estimated one-third of the GDP and about 70%

of total employment in emerging market and developing economies".

One more blot on the current economic blueprint is the incredible collapse in global oil demand and oil prices. Add to that, the emerging political and economic war being waged with China, the second largest economy in the world and perhaps the world's largest trading nation !

Less than two years ago, in 2018, China's combined exports and imports trade tally of $5 trillion, shot past the United States of America to steal the #1 spot, indicating without doubt, China's enormous global trading power and clout in determining the fate of the global economy.

Business leaders will need to consider the impact of this fallout on business, severely disrupting supply chains efficiencies and effectiveness determining market competitiveness driving businesses to the brink of disintegration and death.

It would take a lot of doing to compensate for the gigantic hole this will blow in business strategies of countless businesses across the world. The economic outlook added to the pandemic creates a dark foreboding world, once which shall test the character, spirit and competence of every leader.

Purpose and Meaning in a Dark 2020 World

You have to figure out what is going to get you out of bed with joy and enthusiasm every morning. In a reformatted world, much has changed of the settings you had put into place.

Some are lost or permanently dismantled. A Factory Reset of sorts. It needs you to reboot your drive. The entire hard drive and operating system of your life. With a new software which is always on auto update, catching you by surprise with every update !

The new landscape of life is not a cancellation of everything you did or knew. It is more a reimagined version of life and a new source of energy. The "same old same old" just doesn't fire up the spirit anymore.

This newly harnessed energy drives you right through the challenges of each unfolding day. Of the new way of working and living. It allows you to embrace the challenge of this unusual sense of dealing with something completely new inside the framework of something old and established. Like being presented with new and unusual furniture and radically different interior design in your old apartment.

I am going to quote some extracts from my recent book "Flawed Yet Precious". Because I believe I can put this important aspect of the landscape of work life into the right perspective.

"Personal Purpose has been called many names. It has been called the Lighthouse of life, it has also been called the Goal Posts of life. Whichever way you look at it, Personal Purpose is like the North Star, a star in your Sky which gives you a sense of direction. Most often people are happy with the fullness of life, being occupied with actions that fill up the entire time that they have."

You may have had a good bearing on this before the world turned life upside down. So, you need to get back to your window and look for your North Star again. Maybe it will shine a little differently. Yet as long as you realize your significance in the role you play in leading and living the new mandate of life, you have a head start to getting there.

"There are few ways in which you can look at this. One is look at how the world is and how you wish the world to be. You will probably find that there is a gap between how the world is and how you want it to be. Now look at your life and ask yourself, how can you use your life to fill in that gap. Can you fill in the gap from where you are and what you do? Do you have to stretch from where you are or do something completely new to fill in that gap? Naturally the gap you shall see, is a global gap. It's not really about something locally specific or personal in your life. You may wonder why should purpose be attached to it ? A Global issue ? But that's really the reason why all of us on this earth exist."

"Purpose is born from a compelling reason for the future of our earth and not just a reason drawn from one's personal life. Our lives are funneled into the overall purpose of the planet. You can therefore take things that you are passionate about and see how

they fit in to the purpose that serves the world. It would determine the way you live your life. So the point is, when you are looking at what you want to do what is your heart's desire, with unfettered abandon, not constrained by any of the burdens of life of either finance or time or family obligations and you look at establishing your role in managing purpose, you will find that your passion can help you put in place the stepping stones on the pathway that lead you towards the greater purpose of life."

Where is the Office of Visible Purpose ?

Almost everything physical is now virtual. The office is not just a fixed physical space anymore. Going to work may have changed forever. As a participant of this new way of life, the paradigms have changed sufficiently to displace the sense of familiarity and comfort with the process of doing something as simple as "going to work" or identifying with a place called "the office". It is scary for some to imagine life without the physical trappings of a regular office including the physical presence of people who populate it. The office of visible purpose is invisible !

LEADERSHIP IMPERATIVES

Working From Home during the long lockdown began with joy and soon turned terribly difficult. Because the traditional home is not built around the idea of an office. Segregation and separation of the home from the home-office has tested tolerance, stretched patience and almost torn lives apart. We shall learn to adapt with time, and our resilience will see us through the process of reinventing this significant part of our lives. The images in our mind have to change and that will influence our sense of life. The sheer power of the physical structure of factories and offices, the throb of giant machinery, the gigantic gleaming edifices, the plush decor, the awe inspiring hum of production, the intimidating design of elegant working spaces charged with the electricity of the business, the thick luxurious carpeting of success that shrouds the bare floors of toil and hardship, the adrenaline that rushes through the veins when in the hallways of power and the boardrooms of business, the privileges of being an insider, a citizen of this mini nation, the heightened sense of self-worth just to be part of this immense physical evidence of success.

This is what we unconsciously frame our lives with, when we "go to work". This is how we define ourselves. This is what we transition our lives to everyday , from the ordinariness of our homes to the extraordinariness of our office. The extraordinariness of ourselves. And that may suddenly disappear. With it, disappears that huge anchor of pride, worthiness and esteem we dropped in the deep waters of our lives. Our boat, although afloat is now adrift !

Owning Your Job

Every individual will be an owner of the job. This can be part of a new organizational culture or can even be worked into contracts. In a world where Work From Home or WFH as it is called, is increasingly a preferred option by employers and employees, the role of a manager as a supervisor is rendered redundant.

A manager can now free up her time to add more value to the deliverables rather than chasing people to show up with their work as required.

Owning your job, literally means you are a business partner-owner of your role and salaries turn into cheques you get to write. Based on mutually agreed metrics. It may sound complex right now but if worked on, can solve several problems including feeling invisible, underutilized, overworked, overlooked, robbed of credit, working on other peoples' goals and deliverables, especially those of the boss, owning up to mistakes and losses, earning on effort, criticality of deliverables, rewards for added value, alignment with the organizations goals, living key identified values of the company in demonstrable ways. This is the new face of the office of our future.

Not just the Leadership, but everyone, must own this and make it possible. We shall have to work on organizational design and people management with a zeal and effort that is just as much, if not more, as we have worked on technology.

Technology must serve the people it was built for. Not the other way around.

PART TWO

NEW SCRIPTS OF SUCCESS

You are not in the universe, you ARE the universe, an intrinsic part of it. Ultimately, you are not a person, but a focal point where the universe is becoming conscious of itself. What an amazing miracle

Eckhart Tolle

Part Two
New Scripts of Success

Chapter Four
Clarity of Now

Chapter Five
Competence for Tomorrow

Chapter Six
Commitment to Change

CHAPTER FOUR
CLARITY OF NOW

Energizing Every Moment

If there is anything that we have learnt from the 2020 crisis, it is this. That we have no idea if we will live beyond the moment we are in. There is no guarantee at all that we would be able to see the end of the day or the end of the week of the end of the month or even the end of the year. The global pandemic has claimed lives in an unbelievable manner. The statistics are mindboggling. Lives have become numbers in those statistics. People who lived and dreamed like each one of us.

The world is indeed facing a crisis of incredible proportions. We have never ever witnessed such a time in our lives, at least for the past 100 years.

LEADERSHIP IMPERATIVES

Where nothing is guaranteed. Everything that was isn't the way it used to be and nobody seems to have an idea of what the future shall be. The only thing we have is the moment we live in and therefore it is really important that we appreciate every moment we have and make the best use of it.

That is the reason why we have to energize the moment we have. To put all our energy, positive energy, into the moment we live and do anything that we can to support life in the moment, living as fully as we can.

The world of work too will witness people who value the moment more than ever before. To create a future too, which can guarantee life and all its trappings. Because we have witnessed great loss already. So, a leader of the New World beyond 2020 would have to bring as much energy into the moment as possible to meet those expectations, expectations which are much sharper, as they arise from severe loss, not just desire.

No one really can predict how the world is likely to

turn. No leader too really knows what awaits humanity in the future and therefore whatever we can do in the present moment has to be something significant. Something which will both live in and invest the present.

Which means we've got to ask ourselves this. Can we really live life fully in the moment without being too concerned about how we are going to survive in the future ? Naturally everything we do in the moment will have a bearing on what happens in the future.

When we look at opportunities and relationships and engagements with the current moment it could well be that we find new treasures that are lying right in front of our eyes. Within easy reach as compared to the treasures we seek in the future, which are neither in sight nor within easy reach.

The only way to create a significant tomorrow would be to live today as well as we can.

When one goes to work, we have to look at what kind

of engagement we would like to have in the moment, what kind of relationships would be like to create in the moment, what kind of business momentum we can create in the moment.

So, every customer you meet is valuable in the moment, every colleague you work with is valuable in the moment. Every relationship that you have needs to be protected in the moment, nurtured and grown in the moment.

Tomorrow will come but that tomorrow will truly be based on what you do today.

Creating Presence

The best way you can enjoy the moment you live in is to create presence in that moment. To expand your consciousness to fill that moment. Each and every moment.

Presence is about being hugely present, being witness to your own life in the moment. To be able to be in the moment and yet outside the moment as an observer. To be able to live fully in the moment and yet at the same time be able to be witness to how you live that moment and to use that experience to give yourself some kind of silent advice on what you need to be doing better.

My suggestion to you is this. As you create presence in as many moments of your life as you can, you will find that you are able to understand more about the way you live, how you live each moment and what you can deliver in that moment.

When we talk about the moment, we're not really just talking about every second, every minute or every hour that we live in. While of course it does mean that, it really is about how much time we really expect to be able to devote to what we are doing.

So, don't put anything off for tomorrow if you can do it today. Reach for greatness today rather than put it off for tomorrow. If you can be available to yourself or others today then do that. If you can write a book today, do that. If you have the urge to learn painting, do that today. If you can secure a business deal today do that. Or do as much as you can to secure today something that will almost inevitably follow tomorrow.

We have been living lives deeply invested in ourselves, and not truly for the future of the planet or human life on it. The entire time we've consumed in the moment has not even really been about gathering steam for the future.

We would learn much better through creating presence in the moment. To be witness to the future in the present moment. And that is what is great about creating presence.

So, live and demonstrate in the moment, what you value and believe in, what you live for, to be your own greatest ambassador for a powerful present and a future which mimics that moment.

Eyes Wide Open

The steady rhythm of a set life, often has us sleepwalking through it. Especially when we have reached seniority in our careers or expertise in our field of work. Or, we are led by the eyes and sight of people we trust to see the world better than we can.

This happens when we are young students, young employees and young in our careers.

It's amazing how a rude awakening is what it takes to open our eyes wide. And this is exactly what has happened. Not to just a few. But to the entire world.

Unfortunately what we have seen in this rude awakening has been quite terrifying. Suddenly we are brought to painful levels of awareness of the state of our lives. How unfinished, or poorly equipped, or how low on quality, or how disabled it is for delivering on our dreams. For some of us, this awakening has come too late. But for the rest of us who shall see this year through, it means we are never going to sleepwalk through our lives ever again.

Never again shall we be led by the eyes of others. We have to promise ourselves to live and lead our lives, with our eyes wide open. And help others do that too. Especially as leaders in this new landscape of life

The greatest triumph of leading life successfully beyond 2020, would be valuing the individuality of people we work with, their diversity which often sees the same world with different eyes, their unique interpretations, opinions, points of view, varied skills and competencies.

Suddenly the dark warehouse of our life shall have more than a hundred thousand torches shining their light.

Think of life like a giant blank wall. Now imagine that everyone holds a torch which projects an unique design of their minds and lives. If we get everyone to switch their torches on, we would get chaotic mixes of designs. And then, when we offer each design safe space on life's wall, well, we get this glorious richly textured landscape.

Learning to swap spaces with others can produce the most magical, mesmerizing, moving landscape as the designs dance across the wall of life to keep creating and recreating possibilities we could hardly have ever imagined.

That is what we get when everyone is invited to life, with Eyes Wide Open !!

CHAPTER FIVE
COMPETENCE FOR TOMORROW

Touch Tomorrow Today

Even more that before, the ability to predict the needs of the changing landscape of the future would be crucial for communities and organizations to survive and thrive.

Invoking the future into the present is the best practice we can get. The 2020 experiences indicate that we are unlikely to get back to our old and familiar ways. The digital future is already here. Remote working has taken over. Online shopping, online learning, online education is quickly pushing aside the old ways of doing these. It's incredible that we have been so ready for this without having predicted it.

So, reaching into our future dictated by the sheer unpredictability of our current times, we must start living today the realities of our tomorrow. Deliberate disruption is key to not just upturning set ways and mindsets but also preparing a whole new normal of living with the unpredictable.

It's not so much about preparing for the future, as much as, drawing the future right into the present. It may seem odd that we should add to the burden of our current chaos, but we don't have much choice. We have to be storm chasers, rather than wait in fear for the storm to strike.

The exploratory and pioneering spirit of Man has to engage with unprecedented levels of courage and character.

Create the Future

What must be our design considerations as we create our future? If the times of today are any indication, then it seems that these could well be the Paradigms of Future Design:

- Unpredictability of Life. Health Risks - Physical and Mental Living with Danger (virus and other onslaughts)
- Shifted Life Priorities & Focus. New Economics, Econometrics, Tools of Trade New Paradigms of Power- Who holds the Keys?
- Turbulence, change and disruption as constant companions to any plans and strategies we make.
- Radically changed sense of Time, Travel, Entertainment, Relationships, Education Options, Career Choices.
- Transformed Business Mission, Vision, Strategic Intent.
- New and Reordered Drivers of Human Behaviour, including loneliness, depression, desperation, paranoia, suspicion and selfishness. Indicative of our transition from socially secure to asocial threatened lives

What is the kind of world you are prepared and willing to live in ? How would you describe it in as much detail as possible?

How would you embrace these paradigms of change in your life, your relationships, your career choices, your lifestyle, your business? What advice would you give yourself? Who would you consider worthy of giving you advice? What makes them eligible? Is there a lesson there for you ?

It is useful to reflect on these questions in order to consider how you can act on them. So, whatever you visualize of the future, break it down into knowledge, skills, competencies and actions that would need to be taken to meet those needs. From this list, examine what you can work on right away. Don't wait for the future to knock on your door. It doesn't knock anymore. Now it blows the roof away. So, as you create your future step by step today, your future self will thank you for the head start you shall have.

Let's imagine how this can be. While you won't really know all the dimensions of the future, you know for sure that the future is digital. What can you do now to equip yourself to be a digital world player? What kind of readiness are you required to step up to?

As an individual and a leader, the difference is just this. Whatever you want for the people you lead, whatever you are going to get them to do, you must also do yourself. Because this new world doesn't carry dwarfs on the shoulders of giants. There is no room for dwarfs anymore. If you want to build giants, you cannot be a dwarf!

Earn from Churn

We have to set goals to earn from the churn. It is not enough to simply learn. Which we must. And earn from what we learn. Some may feel that it would be very risky and too early to launch revenue streams before the roadmap to the future is designed. That cannot be more untrue. In-fact the truth is, since nobody really can predict what is likely to happen, living in the moment is where life is at. Where business can be grown. Where people would like to engage with progress even if it is unsure and slow.

It's like hopping out of your limousine stuck in traffic and riding a bicycle out of it. You still have wheels. Half of what you had. Yet they move you forward. You may never get your limo back. But the aim was to reach your destination, right? Not luxuriate and die rich in traffic!

What is your bicycle like? What business does its bell ring?

If you look at social media today, it is flooded with everybody earning from the churn. Webinars and Online Certification courses across a variety of skills and competencies. Some new some old. But packaged and sold in new ways.

Naturally you will find the ingenuine and inauthentic too. But that does not really compromise the quality and creativity of a large number of these offerings. The fees are very modest to assist registrations during these times, when a lot of people are paralyzed into poverty; poverty of choices, poverty of optimism, poverty of hope. And rich in despair, desperation and dread.

The very goals of earning from churn is to move from such Paralysis of Poverty to the Power of

Productivity. To know, recognize, acknowledge and employ the life in our limbs, fire in our heart, spirit in our soul, so that we never give up on ourselves or learn to be helpless.

CHAPTER SIX
COMMITMENT TO CHANGE

Change, the only Constant

The scenario we are witnessing is nothing but change in constant churn. Like a turbulent river overflowing its banks and sweeping everything away with it. We can expect the world to constantly deliver on change. It is enormously difficult to know what to expect in this churning world which we are still barely able to understand and come to terms with. To imagine that the changes that are being wrought will stabilize soon is far from reach of the most optimistic mind. Yet the human spirit is determined to get a hold of this, to build new platforms of progress that have now reached a certain level of precarious stability, despite the fact that they are far displaced from where they were.

In the new world we are living in and in which we strive to continuously progress, we can expect that every day will present us with new elements of this change. The fact is that we do not have the virus under any sort of control, six months after it hit us. And it is not expected that we will do so for the next two and a half to three years, the elusive vaccine still awaited.

This is a clear signal that living with change and living with risk, living with danger, living with the temporariness of life, are our new watch words. What do we expect to see every time we get up each morning, that is besides being grateful to get up each morning, when we look out of the window at the world ?

It seems to be pretty much the same as it was the previous day and then we turn on the news and we find that the world has changed dramatically over night. While we slept, the world went through turmoil.

Turmoil unseen and unknown to us and yet affecting hundreds and thousands of lives across the world. While all the horrifying statistics may not mean as much to us as they really are, it takes just one person known to us, to fall victim to this pandemic, for us to realize how real and how close to home this entire situation is.

As we look at what the chances are for surviving and thriving in such a chaotic world of churn, we are sure of one thing. Change is constant and therefore no matter what plans we make for tomorrow they are likely to change because they would not apply any more in the way that they were planned.

So you may want to ask why plan at all ? Why live in the hope that tomorrow will bring something new and manageable to the table of our lives ? Well, we don't know. But we have to have to hope that we will see this through and all that we have to do is learn to live a life that is very different from the way we learned to live our lives earlier.

Where our lives before 2020 were based on stability, our lives now are based on instability. The more unstable the world and the more willing we are to accept the instability of the world and our role in that instability, the better are our chances of managing that instability. To ride the wave of instability, wave after wave, where the instability has no likelihood of providing even the semblance of settling into some kind of stability.

Living in a tsunami struck world, there is only the swirling water and the higher ground of the hills. The only way to the hills is from that swirling water. And the water isn't giving up. We have got to learn to float first.

The Caterpillar Must Die for the Butterfly to Fly !

My first book this year is titled The Butterfly Blueprint. In this book I wrote about managing transformative change and here too, I find the analogy of the Caterpillar transforming into a Butterfly very useful.

So what is the romance of The Caterpillar turning into a Butterfly really about ? Well to begin with, it is not romantic at all. The story of metamorphosis is anything but a happy one. In-fact it is a gruesome story of change. It is about being dragged into change in order to produce something that is truly beautiful at the end of that change.

If however, you were to inform a Caterpillar about the process of change, I am sure that no Caterpillar would sign up for such a change.

It is not up to the Caterpillar to accept or deny the change process, unfortunately. The Caterpillar must die. Nature so decrees. The Caterpillar is born in order to die. The primary purpose of the Caterpillar is to feed itself so that when it dies it can produce a healthy butterfly.

The cocoon is the chrysalis in which this magical and difficult transformation takes place. Today we are looking at a world which is very much like a chrysalis. As caterpillars of this earth and of the old ways of life, we are now being drawn into the messy darkness of the cocoon. The cocoon is the Caterpillar's grave, where everything is destroyed except the original DNA sacs or nascent vessels of butterfly life, that were born with the caterpillar. Which were carried through its life in order to become a butterfly.

If you look at it, this means that everything we did and lived for in the past has to be destroyed. Though, the essence of that earlier life, is what produces new life. So, it does not mean that we lose everything we learned. Our earlier lives hold the keys to the future. We were given these keys when we were born. We just did not know that.

Yes, it does mean that we must lose our identities completely into the grave of the cocoon. As most of us are witnessing and feeling in the time of the coronavirus pandemic it feels as if we are in that cocoon of life. A dark tomb that we have built ourselves and put ourselves into.

We have made an unconscious decision to die and the universe is simply agreeing with our decision. As we go through these times, everyday seems to prove that the things that we practiced in the past can no longer be useful in the way they were. In-fact some of the things that we practiced are exactly the opposite of what is required.

Now our entire way of life or lifestyle, our understanding of the future, the way we interacted with each other, the relationships we forged, the plans we had for life and the strategies for growth. All of these are no longer the ones we can use today. While there are vestiges of what our life was and how it worked, if we really want to deal with the birth of ourselves as butterflies, we have to accept the darkness of death in the cocoon.

Where, in that cocoon, everything that identified with who we were, has to be dissolved into nothingness and from that nothingness shall arise the butterfly that we must be.

What that butterfly is and can do, shall be something that we have to try and understand from a very new perspective. This is going to be difficult because as caterpillars, the canvas of our life was the earth. As butterflies the canvas of our life is the sky. So, there is this huge Earth to Sky difference between who we were and who we are going to be. Naturally we are going to be caught completely off balance.

Our sense of stability and center of gravity is going to be redefined and we shall have a feeling of floating with absolutely no control over our flight. That is, getting used to strapping on Butterfly Wings which take us to the sky.

As soon as we accept acknowledge and embrace the Idea of the Butterfly and the Cost of the Cocoon, only then we shall be able to manage to pay the Price of Change and add wings to the Butterfly !

As leaders, you are Butterflies too. Masters of both, your Cocoons and Skies. Your roles would need you to create, nurture and grow Butterfly Communities. From Caterpillars who shall fight the Cocoon.

Yet as Butterfly Mentors you must engage the process of transformation. To produce Butterflies.

This would need Courage, Compassion and Character. To lead with tough-love, to be an example of the change you advocate, to be

LEADERSHIP IMPERATIVES

vulnerable, to be committed to the sky.

The New Leadership Imperatives which are described in the pages that follow, are what is recommended to mentor and manage this change.

PART THREE

THE NEW LEADERSHIP IMPERATIVES

A true leader has the confidence to stand alone, the courage to make tough decisions and the compassion to listen to the needs of others. He does not set out to be a leader, but becomes one by the equality of his actions and the integrity of his intent

Douglas MacArthur

The New Leadership Imperatives

Chapter Seven
The Warrior Leader
Business Crisis Centered Leadership

Chapter Eight
The Digital Leader
Technology Centered Leadership

Chapter Nine
The EQ Savvy Leader
Heart Centered Leadership

Chapter Ten
The Ignited Leader
Spirit Centered Leadership

In the new normal these are the Leadership Imperatives which shall demand our awareness, attention, application and agility.

None of these truly exist in themselves alone nor do I believe that even together they represent all the answers to the circumstances which assail us. But they are definitely the leadership approaches which shall define the rest of the pathway with a sense of great Purpose.

At different points in time, these Leadership Imperatives can be called on separately or collectively to deal with situations which like the wraiths of the dangerous dark seas, appear to be familiar apparitions of the past, yet conceal the true tides of the waters we are set to sail in.

As you read each chapter, keep in mind how you can connect the characteristics of each Leadership with the one that follows. To join, merge, compensate and especially, to rescue from the danger they pose to themselves.

LEADERSHIP IMPERATIVES

Each Leader walks a dangerous path. A Path which leads into the Darkness of a deeply troubled yet necessary future. To know and appreciate what each type of leadership centered companion can do and achieve, is an enlightenment which can provide protection, balance, alignment, integration and wholesomeness by using Companion Leadership Centering.

Ask yourself, which Leadership mantle you would choose to wear and which would be your Sword, your Scabbard and your Crown

CHAPTER SEVEN

THE WARRIOR LEADER: BUSINESS CRISIS CENTERED LEADERSHIP

The most effective way to live is as a warrior. A warrior may worry and think before making any decision, but once he makes it, he goes his way. To make a million other decisions awaiting him. That's the warrior's way

Carlos Castaneda

LEADERSHIP IMPERATIVES

As the doors of the economy creak open, industry is set to burst through those doors. Though in the melee to get to the sacred alter of business transformation, many businesses are likely to get trampled over, crushed underfoot or stumble to reach just short of grasping the Holy Chalice of Change.

The challenge is to stand up and hit the ground running. Though getting up itself is difficult, on creaky limbs with rusted unoiled hinges, from the long cooling period of lockdown.

Developing New Emergent SWOT (Strengths Weaknesses Opportunities Threats) based integrated business strategy plans to function on real time data. To blow holes in the haze of this holdup, to see some signs of vitality on which these business plans can be hinged.

This is possible when organizations develop the prowess of Warrior Leadership, when the world has convulsed its way into a grim battlefield.

The Warrior Leader is the King of the Jungle. Agile, Bold, Brave, Competent, Connected, Dynamic, Decisive, Energized, Fearless. One can go on.

Though the other important ones which matter on the battle ground are Visionary, Resilient, Versatile and above all Lethal.

Let's look at these four aspects of a Warrior Leader.

The Visionary Warrior

The Resilient Warrior

The Versatile Warrior

The Lethal Leader

The Visionary Warrior

Future focused with the uncanny ability to have a 360degree perspective of situations. High level anticipatory strategies support the vision. The Visionary Warrior can sense both danger and opportunities way ahead of others.

It results in a honed level of preparedness which can surprise others who haven't picked up on the cues and signals from the same environment. Which when sensed and stitched together through multiple interpretations connected to the design of the future, allow the Visionary Warrior to appear to have 360degree vision and actions that seem to be timed with the skill of a soothsayer.

The pitfall to be watched for could be awkward stumbling blocks thrown up by reality checks of the present moment. Like taking some of the current resources including people for granted, in the rush to reorganize the future.

The Resilient Warrior

Adversity is the sparring partner of a Resilient Warrior Leader. It provides such a leader with opportunities to constantly learn on the run and roll with the Punches.

Resilient leaders don't hold grudges as they consider every act of adversity as an opportunity to discover new possibilities. Of growth and progress. Optimism shines brightly like the sun in a cloudy sky. It is this along with the ability to be a great problem solver that takes organizations through dark and tricky times.

With vast reserves of positive energy of self-belief, self-confidence, self-worth and emotional self-awareness, such leaders constantly find the

"Possible in the Impossible"! A Resilient Warrior Leader may at times appear to fail to acknowledge how much of a beating a business can take. They appear to push the limits beyond breaking point.

Which may create resistance from within the organization to support buy-in to strategies proposed and serve as drag and delay to their successful implementation.

Diplomacy, Conflict Management, Negotiation Skills and a Sense of Humour add to the ability to roll with these punches too.

The Versatile Warrior

Agility is key to success. Such leaders are constantly engaged within the organization and industry, and are capable of provoking and invoking change. Innovation and adaptation sit at the strategy table of the Versatile Warrior.

The SWOT Map like an App is constantly updated to its newest version. The Versatile Leader is a vital part of the Leadership Triumvirate with Visionary and Resilient Leaders.

Versatility not only feeds these leadership plans with business data spread and depth, but also, agile strategies employing innovation and adaptability to support business in what may seem to be end-of-the-rope choiceless times. With Versatility at the business strategy table, the business will always benefit from toning its strategic athleticism rather than just muscularity.

Versatility can sometimes excessively consume resources in experimenting with innovative choices. Pragmatism is a good companion to Versatility in order to keep it real.

The Lethal Leader

This is perhaps the most fearsome warrior leader of all. Laser like Vision which cuts right through the clutter of chaos, unerringly seeks and finds the Vision under siege and its assailants.

This Warrior has profound clarity and presence, honed on the frontlines of the business battle field. Whether it is in the boardroom or the marketplace itself. The approach is direct, hands-on and with little time for diplomacy.

The Lethal Leader is a powerful Warrior, knowledgeable, skilled, action driven and yet a super strategist. Always playing to win. The advantage of this Lethal Warrior is a razor-sharp mind, which is quick to spot and leverage strategic business opportunities and loopholes as they appear.

There is very little waiting time in such brief windows and so consequences are faced at super speed too. The skills of Agile, Versatile, Resilient organizational leadership will be vital in responding swiftly. Visionary Leadership will keep Lethal Leadership in check and in service to the Vision of the organization.

The Lethal Warrior Leader is not always invited to the Triumvirate Leadership table, but is always on call. Short on diplomacy and patient parrying in negotiations, the Lethal Leader can be volatile and disruptive.

Yet in chaotic times of extraordinary change as we are witnessing today, disruption is already in play. This is the battlefield where this warrior leader thrives.

LEADERSHIP IMPERATIVES

While we have examined each of these four dimensions separately, they form part of the integrated competencies of the Warrior Leader. The four faces of leadership in disruptive times.

As you can see, the New Leadership Imperatives arising from the ashes of 2020, must begin with the Warrior Leader!

At an organizational level, let's look at what according to me, could be the operating framework of the Visionary, Resilient Versatile and Lethal Warrior Leader

I like to view it through the framework which emerges from the anagram PURCHASE

P : Powerful Purpose

U: Unique Value Creation

R : Rainbow Reasoning

C: Change Ready

H: Hardwiring Purpose to the Vision

A: Arming an Agile Organization

S: Super Skilling

E: Engaged Partnerships

P: Powerful Purpose

This is the Lighthouse in the turbulent seas of disruption. It cuts through the fog to give you a sense of direction. Purpose fueled by passion to sail the seas no matter the weather is a lethal combination of elevated levels of reward and risk in radical times.

Yet putting the Light of Purpose to shine brightly enables leaders clear the path to fulfill those crucial elements of the organization's overarching goals. Goals which determine its very existence.

It facilitates the organization push heavily against key identified constraints and barriers that block or impede the pathway to defined purpose. This must be experienced at an individual level first and then the collective determination of such individuals can lead the organization forward together.

A Warrior Leaders must lead an army of Warrior leaders, inspired by powerful collaborative purpose

U: Unique Value Creation

The need of the hour today is the creation of unique value. Value that is acknowledged and recognized in the market and chosen repeatedly and widely for it. When the market is looking at what to spend their dwindling, scarce and barely replenishable resources on, it's really important to give them a wildly compelling reason to choose you.

Leaders need to have the clarity of purpose and the courage prune and shape the organization's product offering to clear the debris of complex and complicated product packaging, extensions, modifications, morphing and other disguises, to let the market know what special engine drives the car. It's like putting the engine on the hood rather than under it.

Naturally what you expose shall be examined. Thoroughly and critically. It has to be more than adequate. More than useful. More than satisfying. It has to be electrifying. Set pulses racing. Create a new playing field altogether.

A Warrior Leader of 2020 & Beyond must have this Battle Blueprint always in play. All the old landscapes have altered radically as we have read earlier. Needs have altered radically too.

Businesses which choose to market solid and sound old offerings to this radically altered world, will no longer find themselves viable. Black, White & Grey Mindsets need to employ Rainbow Reasoning produced by the sunlight of new thinking refracting through the prism of unique value.

R : Rainbow Reasoning

The Seven Colour Spectrum Rainbow of Reasoning is Thinking which has the Colours of Feelings. Emotions drive behaviour and business.

Clinical Black, White & Grey Strategic Thinking needs to move to Rainbow Reasoning. To read, understand and incorporate feelings and emotions into product portfolios, business decisions, and organizational development.

Rainbow Reasoning brings in multi-dimensionality to become useful tools of the Visionary, Resilient and Versatile leader. The different aspects of how different stakeholders of the organization view the vitality of the company, colours every situation and gives Leadership the opportunity to see more of the landscape, recover quicker, relate more to choices and identify with the emotional drivers of the business as they present themselves. This increases ability and agility of leaders to manoeuvre the organizational response both outside and inside the organization.

VIBGYOR are the Colours of the rainbow. Each colour can be assigned significance within the organization and conversations can use such colour driven vocabulary to express a whole range of thoughts, feelings and choices which accompany each colour. Don't forget to include Black and White too!

Let's do a quick exercise. We shall, just for the purpose of this exercise, identify each colour with a primary flag of thought and feeling.

V : Violet : Deep, dark and intense, rich with hidden information, muted expression. Aristocratic, so doesn't seek acclaim. Runs the risk of being overlooked.

I : Indigo : Deep yet bright, with an inner glow of priceless worth, expressed cautiously. Catches the eye with the quiet wealth of its character.

B: Blue: Sparkling, bright, refined, distinguished. Unmistakable open sky culture.

G: Green: From the Houses of Blue and Yellow but with its own significant presentation. Has earthy intensity, depth and calm controlled energy. Reflects new life and growth.

Y: Yellow: Bright, cheerful, radiant, produces feelings of happiness and joy. Lights up life, like the sun. Soothes the soul like buttercups in bloom. Vibrates constructive energy in flow.

LEADERSHIP IMPERATIVES

O: Orange: Bright, intense, high energy, announces passion, emotional arousal and rush. Attracts immediate attention and has magnetic appeal.

R: Red: Fiery, bold, outstanding, deep and bright, strident character, unbridled emotion both positive and negative, signals both attraction and danger. Celebratory and catastrophe.

B&W : Black & White : Black is Deep, Dark and Foreboding, White is Bright and Blank. Between these two, a lot of open doors have been shut, the ambiguous shaped into definite form, the unwritten put down as written into finality.

Separately they have their own different contexts, one, a bold definitive statement etched with dark outcomes, the other with an open approach, which begs to be closed. Like a blank paper almost calls out to be printed upon.

The Black defines itself on White. The White contrasts the Black. Together they have ruled the Thought-driven Mind. It's time they had the Company of Colour.

Now to complete the exercise, take any product you know well as a consumer of that product. Put down all Colours from Most Representative to Least Representative of the Product, according to you. Circle the Primary Colour or Colours which prompts you to choose it from amongst its competitors. Write your reasons why. Now ask a few others to do the same exercise. Give them the colour code and interpretation.

Compare notes. Or rather Compare Colours. How different are they/ What does it say for how the product is perceived by others? If you were to produce and market this product what would you change about it (Product and Positioning) such that the colours influence making it a sure-sought choice of purchase by an enlarged target market. The colours that emerge may turn out to be quite different from the colours originally charted! How does that impact your thinking? What does it do to the ability to create market leadership? What does it mean if the PRODUCT is YOU? As a Leader?

That's one way of putting Rainbow Reasoning to work! Rainbow Reasoning can be used across the entire spectrum of organizational design-thinking and decision making. Relationships and life decisions too can benefit from the rainbow.

LEADERSHIP IMPERATIVES

C: Change Ready

Invoking and embracing change is a good way to usher in a state of change readiness. Waiting for change to come knocking or even hiding from it, thinking that change in a few somewhat "distanced neighborhoods" won't affect yours, is inviting trouble to your business. Remember the far away China and it's economic impact on every business in the world?

Preparedness of course does not insulate you from suddenness, unpredictability, radical nature and severity of a change storm. But it will help you survive it and hit the ground running when it diminishes. Like right now, we are still in the gale force of the wind buffeting the world.

If you were to read the news accounts of organizations weathering the storm, what would you pick up as signals of their change readiness? Are they business and morale boosting? Or only business boosting? Or business busting?

Downsizing of people, redesigned roles, reinvented business strategy across business product lines, recalculated market focus, resource reallocation, technology transitioning, people re-skilling and such are common signals. Are they about readiness for change or reaction to change? I think the latter, though many organizations would like to label it Change Response.

No matter what you call it, if it brings the organization and its business to shuddering halts or seems like driving with the brakes on, well, that's not readiness for change or change friendly organizational design.

Change Readiness must be examined when all of these are done as part of a continuous business health management process prior to change onslaughts and tuned into the change process when it hits. And yes, there are now many businesses steadily flexing these muscles on an ongoing basis.

Most global and multinational businesses are in advantageous positions to do this, due to their Rainbow Reasoning across different world cultures, geographical imperatives, demographic differences, economies of shortage to abundance, preferences, buying behaviour, driven by these along with Socio-Cultural interpretations and dictates. Best practices and learning curve lessons learned "locally" can transfer their wisdom in reasonably shorter time across such organizations. Making them "Glocally" Responsive and Resilient to change.

H: Hardwiring Purpose to the Vision

Management books define Mission and Vision Statements quite commonly like this. "A Mission Statement describes the company's business, its objectives and its approach to reach those objectives. A Vision Statement describes the desired future of the company"

When the Mission and Vision Statements are put together, they serve to provide a statement of the company's Purpose, Goals and Values. What the Company stands for, Why it exists, Where the company is now, Where it wishes to reach and how it plans to get there.

Purpose is what drives an individual, communities, relationships and organizations. Purpose brings meaning and direction to our efforts and engages our dreams and aspirations which form the Vision we have for our future selves. The same is with organizations,.

When we can see how our reason for living (purpose) delivers our dreams and aspirations (vision) we draw strength from this. We add fuel to the fire inside ourselves, willingly put in the energy and effort, are patient with the process, stay engaged with each step, and form an everyday plan to live that purpose and vision.

An everyday plan of practicing small parts of the future, so that we create ongoing experience, competence and patterns of practicing the alignment to those goals. Along with the safety of values we honour, because incremental daily progress doesn't throw in sufficiently large hurdles that can often severely challenge our values and beliefs.

A Warrior Leader leads with that purposeful vision, learns to be resilient to surmount incredible challenges and setbacks, and practices flexibility and adaptability to reach the desired goals. Everyday. Step by Step. Learning to bend in the storms of disruption and yet not break.

LEADERSHIP IMPERATIVES

A: Arming an Agile Organization

An agile organization is used to describe organizations which are nimble and quick to respond to changes in the marketplace or environment. It is as you just read all about incorporating and leveraging Powerful Purpose, the Creation of Unique Value, replacing Black, White & Grey Thinking with Rainbow Reasoning and Change Readiness to support Change Response.

As you now know, the agile organization uses the effectiveness of Unique Value Creation along with Rainbow Reasoning, to land on its customer's customized needs. To go past satisfaction right up to delight. Instituting a laser like focus on what is called "Customer-centricity" and complete the circle of Creating Unique Customer Centric Value Arming Agile organizations helps them embrace the turbulence and disruption of constantly changing circumstances. In 2020 , peering beyond the food of the pandemic, I can assure you that no one really knows what the market will look like in 2021-2022

Armed Agile organizations are more likely to survive and thrive crossing this dark business abyss. By making decisions quickly, pivoting adroitly on the fulcrum of change, yet remembering to maintain their customer-centric focus.

So, successful Agile Organizations must learn to BE Agile through Powerful Purpose and Hardwiring that Purpose to Vision, invoking and Embracing Change and remaining Customer-Centric to create unique value to products and services delivered.

A Digitally Driven Agile Organization takes Agility to Systems and Processes. In the creation of software driven data chomping intelligent systems which use agile processes to manage critical business deliverables. There is more on this in the chapter following this note, on The Digital Leader.

S: Super Skilling

Super Skilling is honing both edges of a razor-sharp sword. To make it lethal. It means the swordsman must not just be competent by extraordinarily skilled. And extraordinarily informed about the consequences of its use.

LEADERSHIP IMPERATIVES

Why would a leader need to be a Lethal Super Skilled Warrior? There are a few key reasons: a) The severity of circumstances demands that the leader leads the charge from the front. A front-line warrior leader is the first to fall if not super skilled. b) The complexity of the situation needs the leader to rely on personal knowledge, skill and dexterity to recognize problems and implement solutions. Even if competent teams are engaged in the process. c) Authority and responsibility finally lie with the leader who must make sharp, smart and sound decisions at great speed.

Decisions, some of which, shall impact the organization at deep levels and even threaten core values and purpose. These lie in the foundation and at the summit of the organization. Only a super skilled leader shall have the ability to succeed.

Super Skilling is about taking every critical business skill to levels of high competence. In a way, this is what entrepreneurs need to build to be self-reliant and not have to hire expensive business managers to build and grow the enterprise. You know the fate of such entrepreneurs. Or the miscarried careers and fortunes of fallen celebrities.

They are often cheated, misled or badly advised by such managers who destroy the enterprise from within. Let the Warrior Leader take charge of the battlefield. The War is then worth winning!

E: Engaged Partnerships

I have written more on this in the chapters that follow. More specifically under The Ignited Leader : Co-creating the Collective Dream and Collective Partnerships. I would rather prefer you read about it there, but nevertheless, here is an extract which can help you anchor your thoughts in the moment and also serve as a preview of what is to come.

"Co-creating the collective dream is a step on the ladder of collaboration and partnerships. It is about making a pact between the business and the people who drive that business. A pact which is one not just about cooperation but one of collaboration. Collaboration means partnership. Investing everything that you have in the business. Not in terms of money but in terms of emotional equity, in terms of effort, energy and engagement. Dreams and aspirations too must be part of the partnership. A

LEADERSHIP IMPERATIVES

partnership plan where personal agendas of partners merge with the collective agenda to deliver against the overall agenda of the organization."

With PURCHASE, the Warrior Leader Purchases the permission to lead the business through turbulent times. We need to give that permission today.

CHAPTER EIGHT
THE DIGITAL LEADER: TECHNOLOGY CENTERED LEADERSHIP

In today's era of volatility, there is no other way but to re-invent. The only sustainable advantage you can have over others is agility, that's it. Because nothing else is sustainable, everything else you create, somebody else will replicate

Jeff Bezos, Amazon Founder

LEADERSHIP IMPERATIVES

The transformation of life and business today has an unmistakable digital fingerprint. The recent months since March 2020 have been witness to this. Stranded in the lockdown, life has had no alternative except to turn digital. Fortunately, technology had already raced to an advanced level of preparedness to take on the paralysis of the pandemic. Social media, television, the internet of things, the entire magic of life is literally commandeered by our fingertips. The release and relief of the chained human spirit through numerous digital applications has been so spectacular on an everyday level of life, that we have already begun to accept it as the new normal.

Almost every waking moment has been engaged with this flourishing digital world. We are well and truly living a digital life.

At an organizational level, this would mean that business success will be determined by the organization's digital prowess. Led by the organization's Digital Leadership.

What makes an effective digital leader ? Such an individual must be up to speed with the business' goals and must clearly understand how their role and job responsibilities need to dovetail with processes which support achieving these goals.

A digital leader's mandate would be to explore, recommend and institute technology which must be aligned to the needs of the business. The objective must be to not just bridge gaps but also become sharply responsive to the needs of their customers along-with the ever-changing business requirements causing churn and chaos with the relatively older and more inflexible systems and processes.

Digital Leadership needs to usher in a digital savvy culture. A culture which supports digital transformation of all the critical business processes.

At the nuts and bolts level, or rather the basic binary level of understanding and implementing this, it means that digital transformation would need to continuously engage, understand, adapt and apply new and quickly metamorphing digital technology. Which is the equivalent of inviting rapid change at core levels of the business. It's a huge but necessary risk which must be taken and managed on the fly !

LEADERSHIP IMPERATIVES

So you may ask me why digital leadership is so crucial to business and life beyond Year 2020 ?

To answer that we need to appreciate what effective digital leadership does.

A Digital Leader helps his organization create reimagined and restructured workflow and business processes. These act to balance the objectives of quick provision of products and services through new technology applications along with existing systems and process applications.

This balance between old and new systems is crucial, till the technology transition cycle completes. This transition is based on two vital aspects: firstly, the rapidity of response due to the new digital system, to and from the market and secondly, the process triggers which are set off internally by the market response.

Essentially it is about monitoring and managing the three worlds of the transforming business : the world which was and worked well in the past, the churning world of an unstable present which must be addressed by dynamic process design, and the world envisaged in the near future, which is the ultimate digital process destination .

This must be managed through the engagement and application of cutting edge digitally designed and dynamically managed systems and processes.

So how does committed digital leadership serve the organization? It does the following:

Boosts Effectiveness and Efficiency of crucial business processes through the smart use of digital tools designed to deliver superior results.

Reconnects the Organization

Digital Leadership has to communicate, persuade, influence and implement digital strategies across the business to facilitate the interlinking of elements of the business in the digital blueprint of the organization.

Increases and Improves Business

Crunching business cycle times, without the drag of customer resistance through enhanced customer experiences, is an easy formula for success. Add to that enhanced Customer Reach, Mindshare & Wallet Share achieved by improving customer retention rate, loyalty, repeat business and advocacy.

Improves Customer Experience.

Digital leadership's blueprint engages improving real customer experience in the areas of customer convenience, speed of response to your customers' needs and of course customer care and support which is usually the sharp end of the sword for every business. The greatest gifts to your customer are these three- ease, speed and care.

Therefore, what must a Digital Leader promote to make the organization digital ready and lead the market? The starting point is this:

The Digital Leader would be well advised to develop these competencies and characteristics

An Inspiring Persona

Leadership Persona is said to be a powerful manifestation and sheer presence of leadership which a leader demonstrates rather than advocates. A clear digital vision has to get off the walls and charts and visibly walk the halls. People must see the vision in motion. Only then is it believable.

Strategic Digital Vision must follow Personal Presence. The Vision will Walk and Leap only when Strategy Talks Authentically. Leaders must design a coherent digital strategy which helps people see, understand, accept and support the digital agenda of the organization. They must feel part of it.

Influential Communication

Getting the Buy-In of the Digital Strategy and Agenda, needs powerful, persuasive, persistent and pervasive communication. As a leader it is crucial to realize that every little message counts. Every communication must reveal the digital vision, strategy and agenda. And importantly how much you believe in it.

Authenticity matters. Because it builds Trust.

A digital blueprint which most of the time, has barely any old experiences of success, needs the leap of faith and trust in the leader advocating it.

LEADERSHIP IMPERATIVES

Insatiable Curiosity of an Explorer

The pioneering spirit of the explorer is fed and fueled by an insatiable curiosity. Curiosity's natural companion is Risk. It's not surprising therefore that this combination of appetites doesn't come naturally to everyone. Perhaps that's why Digital Leaders feel challenged when attempting to adapt and blend digital technology. When this appetite is cultivated and harnessed it actually drives the business.

Emotional Self-Awareness

As we grow our digital footprint to the level of Big Data chomping Artificial Intelligence, the need for emotional self-awareness and balance increases. The level of connectivity needed for a pervasive integration of digital footprints today is like never before.

The boundaries that existed between, inside and outside the office have to be redrawn if at all they exist anymore. What was a reliable recourse yesterday is not available today. Let's say, if cash was discontinued completely and buying by paying online was the *only way* to purchase, offering to pay cash on delivery would be meaningless.

Every organizational process slated for digital change is attached with Emotional Strings. I personally prefer paperback books to digital books, only because of the emotions attached to reading these books right through my life and the wonderful memories they hold. However today, I write and publish digital books! Because it is now very personal and impacts me directly.

Digital Leaders would be well advised to reflect on their digital approach, strategic plan and agenda and be genuinely interested in how it may affect others in the organization. This digital emotional mindfulness should ideally become a natural and ongoing practice at every organizational level. It must be a vital part of the conversation of progress.

Socio-Cultural Awareness

Socio-Cultural awareness is the community prism through you as a leader of that community beam your digital vision to the world. It is guaranteed to be quite different when refracted. Because the prism of social cultural context shifts the appreciation and interpretation of what was beamed to what is seen. Even when what is seen was beamed from the same original vision.

The Digital Vision you project as a Digital Leader must include and embrace the common social cultural values needed for its success. When these values are protected the vision has a greater likelihood of being approved and accepted. Suspicions are allayed and trust is gradually built.

Innovation, Change & Risk Management

The hard truth is that the digital landscape evolving rapidly and organizational leadership must live on the cutting edge of technology. Where change is truly a constant.

Leaders must embrace rather than shun new technologies even when it adds to a sense of instability and churn. It's better to venture on stage with butterflies in your stomach and a barely practiced script, versus being dragged into the spotlight half naked, kicking and screaming. That's what is likely to happen as a digitally spooked world jumps into action.

Undoubtedly as I have said earlier too, there are risks involved when as a leader you advocate a digital vision and strategic plan that has no previous evidence of success. Simply because innovation has no ancestry of risk.

In the words of Anais Nin " And the day came when the risk to remain tight in a bud was more painful than the risk to blossom"

The Endgame of Digital Leadership is Business Agility. An agile business employing digital tools can pivot with surprising ease and speed to deal with the rapidly meta morphing environment.

From catching up with the changing customers' needs before they are parked away, designing nimble processes before they turn cumbersome, networking across the organization to capture, share, process and put data usefully to work, delivering on quality, innovation, future fitness, but staying proactively ahead of the curve, by harnessing the lightning speed of digital information processing.

LEADERSHIP IMPERATIVES

Effective Digital Leaders must know the various levels of competence across the business , of peoples' capabilities to deal with the digital vision and strategic plan. There is likelihood of some great people who are key to the business at every organizational level, who could be overwhelmed by the onslaught of a digital storm.

When leaders recognize that their people are just as crucial as technology, it can bring the two together with harmony by continuing to advocate the change but also provide sufficient input and resources to develop people to meet and deliver effectively to fulfill the needs of change.

Business Agility needs people to be equally agile as the technology they engage. With Artificial Intelligence already at the door, new world leadership needs to secure the crucial space of the human resource.

CHAPTER NINE
THE EQ SAVVY LEADER: HEART CENTRED LEADERSHIP

IQ and technical skills are important but Emotional Intelligence is the Sine Qua Non of Leadership

Daniel Goleman

Emotionally Intelligent Leaders know when to display emotions and when to delay emotions

Steve Gutzler

LEADERSHIP IMPERATIVES

Most of us are frontline citizens of the world in the most competitive times of our lives – the 21st Century, Year 2020 !! The Year of Transformative Change !

In these unprecedented demanding, high stress, high expectations and highly unpredictable times, we have to do everything possible to stay afloat, survive and thrive

Leadership in Transformed Business more than ever before needs to be a beacon in the New Ways of a New Volatile Uncertain Unpredictable and Complex Life !

Building Effective Business Relationships to Drive Results , especially in this emergent world beyond 2020 shall need us harness our Emotional Energy in a Powerful and Positive Way.

Where Energy Flows, so does Focus, and vice versa. When we allow the difficulties and differences of our relationships to overwhelm our energy and focus, we drive our decisions through that gauntlet. Often accompanied with ego clashes, errant values and power struggles.

Trust is a major casualty in the process. Relationships are torn apart with conflict.

Hardly the way to direct the energy of people, teams and organizations beyond 2020

THE ROLE OF AN EQ LEADER would be to encourage, build and nurture these two crucial emotionally charged traits in people, besides competence, performance and productivity:

o Accountability and Authenticity

o Engagement with Values and Core Principles that define and drive the Vision

These are easy to agree with but difficult to put into practice. Because it means allowing ourselves to be vulnerable. Whether you are a leader or not, at the individual level, human beings all want the same things and have very similar emotions in play.

EQ has a way of looking "inside the engine", "below the bonnet" or "below the tip of the iceberg" at liberating the human being to search, find, acknowledge, accept and befriend the deepest darkest emotion within oneself. Because it is part of who we are.

As new world leaders, at conscious and unconscious levels, emotions are constantly in flow. Engaging EQ energy to electrify our emotional circuits effectively requires conscious attention and practice. To make choices that question the trigger responses of our habituated behaviour. To suit the needs of a world beyond 2020 framed in the context of the Crisis of 2020

Regardless of the roles you represent at work or in your personal life, how you show up matters.

Whether you are a leader from Marketing or Sales or Customer Service or Finance or Legal or HR or Operations, you are wired to the business of your organization.

Every transaction you make inside impacts the quality of the business delivered outside.

Here is your 2020 LEADERSHIP SIX PACK for High Impact Leadership with the Power of EQ

Meet Yourself to Know Yourself

Emotions play a significant role in your life. They direct your focus and attention to the issues you face and depending on how you manage your emotions , you make effective or ineffective decisions which impact your life and those of others too.

It is therefore important to understand the seat of your emotions - the neuroplastic brain, which transforms with every thought you process.

The Emotional brain is where you can manage and coach your emotions to be more effective, but you need to be emotionally literate - to recognize, label and understand your emotions and the information they contain. When you can "meet yourself" you can get to "know yourself".

This is the very first step towards developing emotional intelligence.

Understand Yourself - Measure Your Strengths & Competencies

Emotional Intelligence is often thought of as a description of your capability to manage your emotions effectively. However, Emotional Quotient or EQ is a measurement of how emotionally savvy you are. This is measured across emotional competencies which indicate what is being measured too. It is important that you work toward developing a wholesome development of emotional competence across all the EQ competencies.

EQ Competencies are most easily understood through the famed Six Seconds' EQ Competencies Model often called the KCG Model of EQ, Where it comprises 3 Key Pursuits: Know Yourself (Awareness of the range of Emotions you experience and Your Patterns of Behaviour) , Choose Yourself (Intentionality and the ability to pause, think about consequences and make better choices while remaining optimistic and motivated) and Give Yourself (Finding Purpose through Contributing with Empathy to the world, what you wish to receive from it. In short, building the world you want to live in)

Understanding the imbalances and shortcomings in your emotional competence make-up can give you great insight why you fall into emotional traps and why you make some decisions you are likely to regret later.

Your areas of strength in your bag of emotional competencies can help you develop your overall EQ savvy-ness by leveraging these strengths of your emotional character. As a leader and Captain of the

Ship, people depend on you to leverage these strengths on the rough seas of emotions.

The 2020 Assault on Life, need to be managed with exceptional emotional skill of those who lead the business and society. This is not the best place for the faint hearted to be in the most terrifying storm of the century. Courageous, Competent Leaders of Character forged in the fires of raging emotions need to lead the charge of humanity into the future

Learn to Navigate Life : Patterns Predict Possibilities.

Life ever more that before is like a choppy and churning sea hurling waves against the rocks or like a foaming whitewater river rushing over the edge into the chasm. We are all in that emotional-water of 2020, learning as we go, how to manage the swirl, heave and pulls of the raging currents of our emotions.

Navigating through your emotions to make the best sense of your life, needs you to have a blueprint of yourself, a kind of mind map of your emotional patterns, habits and compulsions. You can then chart your course through these waters to the safety of your desired destination and achieve the results you seek. Otherwise you risk battering yourself against the rocks of your hijacked emotions or drowning in the churn of an emotionally overwhelmed life.

As a leader you are obliged to help people navigate through their emotional churn too. They are passengers in the ship you steer. Teach them to steer the wheel too. That's where some of the greatest lessons are learned. At the Steering Wheel of Life.

Choose Your Path : Consequential Thinking & Caring

Look before you Leap, Think before you Act ! These are the "pause" buttons you need to hit when you engage emotions in your decision making. Life is full of decisions, little ones, big ones, huge ones and even the decision not to make a decision!

When you "Know Yourself" more, you understand your emotions, recognize their patterns, navigate yourself through them to reach your objectives and keep "Choosing for Yourself", the tools you need to manage and drive your emotional cars.

You need to begin as a learner at the wheel of life and graduate to a mature driver of chance and change, thinking ahead of the traffic of the expectations of other people, planning your route to success.

All the while watching the rear-view mirror carefully as you peer ahead through the windscreen often fogged by the heat of your own and others emotions. The World Beyond 2020 lies just ahead of that fogged windscreen. The Rear-View Mirror reflects the ruins of the lives we once had.

Consequential thinking of what lies ahead and what can happen from the choices you make, is a very useful state of mind to master. It helps clear the mist and fog of emptions and assumptions you may have made, now that reality is presenting itself to you more clearly.

Consequential thinking thus teaches you how to use your emotional competencies to steer clear of trouble and navigate the organization, the business and the people who deliver the dreams of the business, to success.

Lead with the Heart : The Roots of Empathy

Dr. Dan Siegel says that "Empathy comes in many colours. Often you may think of your ability to see from another's perspective as the essence of social savviness. Empathy goes beyond that and is the competence of making others "feel felt by you".

It is a way of sensing if their feelings are in tune with you, and that you can resonate with their own inner life. This emotional empathy enables you to feel close and comforted, to sense that others are connected to you beneath and beyond the logic of rational thinking, and that you are concerned about each other, have compassion for each other's pain and take joy in each other's triumphs."

This makes empathy the vibrant rainbow in the emotional sky of our connected lives.

Give Generously of Yourself : Live & Transform Life Everyday

An anonymous yet apt quote reads "Success in life does not necessarily mean acquisition of wealth. Success in life is said to be a state of being when one can come home at the end of the day satisfied with what one has done, being able to put your head on your pillow and have a sound sleep and ... wake up the next day realizing that you are a happy individual, not only because you have found happiness for yourself, but in the process of one day's work, you have given happiness to your spouse, to your children, to your family, to your neighbours and to the world at large." Can you make this your mission too - to live and transform everyday life , everyday

To act as a Leader, you need to BE a Leader ! The landscape is much larger. A manager manages tasks and can also lead. A leader always leads. At times, from behind. That's because Leadership is an inspiring and influential way of life.

Leadership especially in Post 2020 times, more than ever before, is a Leadership in War ! The War of 2020 ! Where Humanity fought for life and lost. But where Human Spirit emerged and won ! Leadership is now more than just leading. It is about inspiring, influencing and launching people to the Vision and Purpose of the organization and the community.

Let's look at what comprise the characteristics of EQ Leadership 2020 Plus !

LEADERSHIP IMPERATIVES

I believe every Leader needs to embrace an agenda of Everyday Leadership An agenda of everyday engagement. In order to embody the ability to influence and inspire people. As a way of living the truths they proclaim. Especially in the new earth of 2020 and beyond.

Listen & Learn

The truth is in common sight outside. Though it now may be repackaged quite differently. As a leader you shall be sending out several messages, communicating your truths and how they must be held. Pay close attention to what the returning message is saying. Is it close to the message you sent out ? What came back ? Did it surprise you ? How have you received it ? What will you do about it ? What can you learn about the unexpected realities of this new way of life ? How must you adapt your message as a leader?

Engage Emotions (Hearts not just Hands)

People must feel valued and appreciated. Either that or they feel neglected. Hardly anyone can claim effectiveness and agility in performance when the heart is heavy. Neutrality is a myth. Emotions influence, if not direct our actions. Emotions when engaged positively radiate into the environment connecting others to the vision. A critical skill as a leader post 2020 would be to energize emotional engagement of every set of heart and hands in the organization with great coherence with the Vision , and to build value and pride while contributing to it.

Activate & Accelerate

Be the spark and the flame. Let knowledge and skill combine to create new standards of performance. Create competence and capacity. Build a groundswell of good practices and processes which will lift people to the performances they desire to deliver.

Acknowledge effort, Acclaim spirit, Activate competence, Accelerate progress. Build Belief in what can be achieved and sustained.

Develop (others) & Delegate

Holding on to power or position does not define true leadership. Real leaders give away powers, making others powerful too. Leaders don't create followers.

Leaders create more leaders. The King maker versus the King.

There is enough powerful positive available in the world to lift every single human being to their potential. Especially today. Leadership is ever more so about building more leaders. Delegating wisely helps people develop and grow into their power.

A powerful organization is a community of powerful positively engaged people performing to their potential. In unison. With coherence of Hand, Heart and Mind across the Collective Dream being co-created.

Equal ownership is the end-game of matured leadership.

Enlarge the Ecosystem

As leaders we influence the ecosystem we operate in. We can either size it down and make it small, narrow, compartmentalized and confined so its easily manageable. Or we can choose to increase the challenge by opening the canvass to full spread. Reorient roles to break down the barriers of mindsets, of parochial performances, of filtered vision, glass ceilings and partitions. Encourage the spirit of entrepreneurship. Lead people to swim the ocean, not to wade in streams.

Redirect & Reshape

Create a renewed pulsating organization. Be constantly aware of the changed journey and be willing to redraw the map, redirect energies and reshape outcomes to serve the common vision of a dynamic metamorphic organization in step with a constantly evolving living planet. A Planet which just taught the world a sharp lesson in its evolution. And has not yet finished with it.

The times of today and the new tomorrow would demand that every leader must Learn while Leading, Engage Emotions of the people, Act Decisively and Mindfully, Develop People's Potential not just performance, Evolve Personally by pushing limiting boundaries and embrace Risk by learning to Reframe Success outside the boundaries of Fear.

Every Leader must leave forward a Legacy. One that inspires others. To continuously strive to create a worthy world for the generations who follow.

LEADERSHIP IMPERATIVES

An EQ Leader leads with emotional wisdom to help people engage as fully as possible with the energy of their emotions as they interact with an uncertain, metamorphing and unpredictable future. It helps engage the courageous heart and ignited spirit to develop Spirit Centered Leadership !

CHAPTER TEN
THE IGNITED LEADER: SPIRIT CENTERED LEADERSHIP

If your actions inspire others to dream more, learn more, do more and become more, you are a Leader !

John Quincy Adams

Co-Creating the Collective Dream

The 2020 lockdown has produced amazing examples of leadership. If you look at how large Cooperative Housing Societies are being managed, voluntary groups supporting delivery of essentials to senior citizens and the sick, relief for immigrant workers and the poor and several such groups at non-governmental levels.

It is amazing to see how everyday needs in such a terrible crisis, are being met by people who have risen to the occasion and are providing outstanding crisis leadership. Leadership which braved the hardship and dangers of reaching out to people, listening intently to the needs of the community, paying great attention to what is important and also being personally available to those who are in need. Such leaders have not only put together plans of action but also have also led from the front. Some at the cost of their lives.

Paying Attention is a key leadership skill. It is about being keenly interested in what the other person has to say. Imagine how you feel when someone is really listening to you, putting aside all distractions. You feel immensely valued and given the chance, you reciprocate it. Paying attention also needs you to put aside your ego and its constant chatter. The prejudices and judgements which flow from it. As a leader it means so much to convey the message that you are creating significant space for others in your mind. Which means that you are pushing aside your own agenda to make room for that of others. It is probably the only collaborative way to learn what your people truly need from you.

Being Available is as important as Paying Attention. It's not just about being physically available, but crucial to great leadership, is being emotionally available. Especially in these turbulent and disruptive times. As a leader, paying attention is valuable, because you make space in your mind for the agenda and needs of people. It is vital however, to be *emotionally available* to others. Emotional availability is the ability to connect hearts. It is the ability to appreciate with empathy the needs being expressed. Making emotional space for something that you are paying attention to, allows it to anchor more deeply within you.

As a leader it produces a much deeper appreciation than the ability to pay attention with the head , but without emotional attention of the heart.

When you bring these two together, of paying attention and making space in your mind by pushing

LEADERSHIP IMPERATIVES

aside your ego and also allow your heart to absorb the emotional undercurrents that attach themselves to the needs of the people, you allow yourself to become emotionally available. You are able to produce the true spirit of leadership which reflects not only the need to be a leader of the business but also a leader the people can trust and turn to. This is a significant competence of leadership. It is what makes leadership so profound and so important.

When a leader not only leads the business and drives results it is expected that this leader manages the relationships which are needed to drive those results. People need to feel connected to the leader not just to the business.

This is the way leadership helps co-create the collective dream of the business along with the dreams of the people who deliver that business success.

Fierce loyalty is built by leaders who care and deliver on their promises to this collective dream.

Collaborative Partnerships

Co-creating the collective dream is a step on the ladder of collaboration and partnerships. It is about making a pact between the business and the people who drive that business. A pact which is one not just about cooperation but one of collaboration.

Collaboration means partnership. Investing everything that you have in the business. Not in terms of money but in terms of emotional equity, in terms of effort, energy and engagement. Dreams and aspirations too must be part of the partnership. A partnership plan where personal agendas of partners merge with the collective agenda to deliver against the overall agenda of the organization.

When we talk about ignited spirit centered leadership, it is the ability to use the transformative power and charismatic spirit of the leader to influence thinking, decisions and actions of the people.

Collaborative partnerships are a product of such leadership, which invoke devotion to an inspiring vision, where every person in the organization feels that she is a valued partner in the achievement of the organization mission.

No matter the role or function of that person is in the organization, nor the hierarchical level of each person across the organizational pyramid. Everybody feels connected, valued and visible.

A true Ignited Spirit-Centered leader connects the heart and spirit of people with the business itself. It is only natural that when people feel that they are intrinsically connected with the organization and are part of the plan, would they be willing to put their entire effort into delivering the business.

Most of the time unfortunately you will see that people are not sure of whether the organization really values them. No doubt that you may pay them a handsome salary or compensation for their efforts. However, if they do not feel that they own the business and are partners in the collective dream, the likelihood is that soon the energy of their involvement would dissipate, the collective dream fade away and therefore give them reason to look elsewhere.

Losing competent and motivated people is a fallout of poor leadership. Of leadership without spirit. It is unfortunately something we see quite often. Almost as if losing such people is the expected and accepted collateral damage of demanding growth. But there are new paradigms in the new world that is emerging in 2020.

The Pandemic or the "Scare of the Century" has both made people cling for dear life to their jobs and also driven people to look carefully at the options before them. The Long Pause has helped put pressure on the needy and reframed the lives of others. Many now want more from life than simply paycheck driven careers. Regardless of this, everybody wants to feel protected, wanted and valued.

It's therefore not just about putting the collective dream to work, but it is also about recognizing the individual in the organization, the individual dream in the collective.

Making the Invisible Person Visible

Most people live their everyday lives, burdened with responsibilities, with their heads bowed down with the pressures of life, focused on protecting their jobs and careers by steadily contributing to the progress of the organization. Yet are visible to just a few people around them.

Even then, in the growing busyness of life, it appears that after a while, they gradually get invisible. Taken for granted. Even forgotten. Grey people in a grey world.

The ignited spirit centered leader in the world beyond 2020 would need to acknowledge every life that exists in the organization. Especially since we have all learnt in the endless lockdown, how easy it is to become invisible.

To become a statistic in the pandemic count. To feel shut out and shut off from the world. It appears that almost the entire world has spent all these months becoming invisible day by day.

No matter what the energy is within us, the flame of human spirit has diminished rapidly. There is a growing feeling of hopelessness and despair. Of being alone and helpless. Paralyzed and invisible.

Putting People and their Dreams to Work

A successful Leader of Life and Business beyond 2020, would need to make not just the person visible but elevate the dreams of every individual to engage with the Vision of the company. To put the person and their dreams to work towards co-creating a future everyone believes in.

To make it obvious, that people and what they value matters to other people too. Especially to the leadership of the organization.

In a world where Artificial Intelligence is not just knocking but thumping on our doors, the entire threat of invisibility is already looming large. The same old questions from the Computer Age arise. Can man be really replaced by machines? Can natural language be replaced by machine language? Can human intelligence truly be replaced with artificial intelligence?

The answers unfortunately seem to indicate that possibility!

Which would mean that while mankind benefits from this entire digitization of human life to the level of artificial intelligence, the actual living human being, would find less and less of a role to play. And therefore spirited leadership of 2020 and beyond would need to elevate human life to a level at which it just cannot be ignored.

Your task as a leader of the New World beyond 2020, would be to make the human being, human life and human spirit the very center of every work design.

To be the center of life, because the human being is that life

Ignited Spirit-Centered Leadership is not just about holding aloft a blazing torch of life and human spirit to light the lives of each individual in the organization or in the community. It is about each person lighting a blazing torch of their own human spirit and purpose.

To build a community of burning torches, a community of human spirit aflame with powerful purpose. To recreate a new earth, taught and shaped by the lessons learned, to make human life thrive and flourish. No matter what the world decides to throw at mankind.

To reimagine this world, it is important that the ignited spirit centered leader lives in every single person and sets their spirits aflame. That flame is what will be needed to carry every single life across the threshold to the future.

LEADERSHIP IMPERATIVES

WHAT REALLY MATTERS

A Leader's Legacy

I can hardly wait for tomorrow; It means a new life for me each and every day

Stanley Kunitz

The true legacy of leadership is building a community of leaders. Especially in the times of today and the abnormal normal. Our world-scape has been sharply redefined by the Pre 2020 and Post 2020 divide.

In-fact while we know that 2020 has cut the world into an almost BC-AD schism, we still do not know what the Post 2020 holds in store for humanity.

Organizations cannot survive in such times by casting leadership into a governing wheelhouse while the rest of the organization waits with baited breath to follow the lead. The times we are in are far too overwhelming and wide spread across every element of life, for leadership to be restricted to a few at the top.

The New Landscape of Collaborative Partnerships, Co-Creation of Collective Dreams, Owning the Job and Paradigms of Transformative Change Leadership as you have just read, are part of a leadership redesign. Where all elements at all levels of the organization redefine their roles to participate in leadership.

What really matters is that we must create every day a better, nobler, happier world than the previous day. An equitable world, of equality across race, creed, colour, religious beliefs, life choices and organizational hierarchy. Everyone must have the right and dignity to be seen, heard and acknowledged.

LEADERSHIP IMPERATIVES

Everyone must live in the light, not in the shadows. Leaders can and must influence that. A whole community of leaders, can actually make it happen. Because leaders own the business. And the business of life is the biggest business we could ever be tasked to lead.

As has been discovered right through the Lockdown on Life, almost nothing else matters more than life itself. Yet to sustain that life we have to get busy with the means to life. We no longer can just live off the land as our caveman ancestors did.

We have developed and are attached and even addicted to the lifestyles we have created for ourselves. While we may have many opinions on this, the fact remains that our creations and inventions have taken us to enormously advanced levels of life and lifestyle.

Now that we are here, we cannot suddenly turn off this life support. Nor can we learn how to live without it, simply because we have evolved and transformed beyond what even we could imagine possible.

Fifty years ago, I was 5years old.

In these 50years our world has evolved meteorically. From tuning into the very few broadcasting stations on the radio, the world has jumped to ushering in an explosion of the super-connected internet of things. Television channels by the thousands are beamed across space directly into a variety of devices, life is connected across the globe in micro-moments via satellites, telephones routinely come with video cameras, complex office software and gigantic storage, carried in pockets or worn on the wrist. Medicine and medical devices serve to extend life way beyond the scourge of disease and even terminal affliction.

Today the unexplored Universe and Space is just another backyard of mankind. It's not just planes that fly with hundreds of people on board and tons of cargo, but also thousands of satellites in space whizz above our heads every day. Supercomputers, software programs driving almost every conceivable device, digital information technology and artificial intelligence form our everyday conversations.

Should we give all that up? Just because we didn't spend the time to learn how to also live in compatibility with such advanced ways of life ? Obviously, No !

We must focus on these Leadership Imperatives to live and lead life beyond 2020. Though we must remember the origin of the life we wish to lead. It literally began with the very first step we took, vulnerable, unsure, fearful yet filled with anticipation, discovery and joy. That became most part of our lives as we grew into our dreams.

Yet, along the way, we have forgotten most of what life truly meant to us, before the pandemic hit us full in the face and knocked us sprawling. All we have to do, is learn about that life now, in the time we have been given. The Universe has paused life so that we can catch up. Let's not lose the opportunity.

As leaders of our lives and influencers of the world, the goal is to bring the Vision of the Future everyday to work, and take it home everyday to our families and communities.

The Imperative is to build a thriving new earth, one which matters to each one of us. For that we need to *tell ourselves in ways we shall never forget, what really matters.*

AFTERWORD

by Pushkar Gokhale

Vice President, B2B and Head, Enterprise Business Security Solutions Division, Godrej & Boyce Mfg Co Ltd., INDIA

The Covid-19 crisis has thrown a lot of Fundamental Questions at us- about Survival & about our Existence. Questions which no one had ever anticipated in their wildest of dreams.

How does one respond and emerge as Winners in these Challenging times? How do we Adapt to the New Normal? Do we focus on Here and Now? Or Do we look ahead?

Through this book Dexter has addressed these Questions in a lucid, simple and effective manner. He has covered a much wider spectrum by not just addressing the Professional side but goes on to explain how Life is changing on the Personal front as well.

The crisis shall have a lasting impact on Study, Career as well as on the Work front. How would one embrace these paradigms of change in life, relationships, career choices, lifestyle and business?

The importance of new Leadership traits in these times of disruption and the PURCHASE Framework are great learnings. All this backed up with Digital enablers and EQ Savvy Leadership is a great recipe for Success in this continuously evolving New Normal.

It's about Re-imagining our Life in the Post Covid Era. As one stares at a highly dynamic & uncertain environment, Dexter has had to put in his visualization to work & bring out the vital aspects of how the VUCA world will playout and how one should quickly transform & adapt to WIN

Pushkar Gokhale

Vice President, B2B and Head, Enterprise Business Security Solutions Division, Godrej & Boyce Mfg Co Ltd., INDIA

Pushkar Gokhale is a veteran result oriented, decisive Leader with proven success and track record involving both Start up as well as Growth Organizations involving Strategic positioning for a Multimillion Dollar Business Unit.

He has built the business and thought leadership by thinking ahead while crafting and mentoring the strategic positioning of the business.

LEADERSHIP IMPERATIVES

ABOUT DEXTER

Professionally Certified Coach (Results Coaching Systems @ 2008- International Coach Federation certified & Professional Coaching Certification @ Coaching Lighthouse @ 2019)

Internationally Certified ENNEAGRAM Personality Profiling @ **2009**(Certified by Jerome Wagner)

Internationally Certified Emotional Intelligence Practitioner, EQ Vital Signs Consultant, Certified EQ – Assessor & Coach @ **2010, 2011, 2012, 2013** (Certified by Six Seconds , California)

Internationally Certified MIND Practitioner @ **2016 (** Certified by MyBrain International Limited, UK**)**

DEXTER J VALLES

A Profile

An International Business Professional, a Life & Executive Coach, *Acclaimed Corporate Master Trainer & a Professor of Management Studies* , across an extensive career founded over an absorbing 32 years with Global and Indian markets

Dexter is considered one of India's leading EQ consultants, specializing in the crucial area of *neuroscience based Emotional Intelligence EQ competencies* applied to Life & Leadership. He is a multi-certified EQ Practitioner, EQ Assessor and Organizational EQ Vital Signs consultant helping people and organizations connect life & work competencies to hidden behavioural drivers

Coaching has been a pursuit of passion for the past 10 years, ever since certifying as a Coach first in 2008. The desire was to enable people reach their goals way beyond the *"classroom of learning"* into the streets of life and the aspirations at their workplaces.

Empaneled as Lead Learning Facilitator, over 20 years Dexter has facilitated and coached dreams and desires, developing competence of several thousands of participants across the globe through innumerable training workshops with several key Indian and Multinational Corporate Houses

LEADERSHIP IMPERATIVES

Dexter's VIDEO Talks

We invite you to watch these interesting videos

Perceiving Reality
https://youtu.be/fG4kGk_IOiA
Perception and Reality are often debated to understand what's really true. Is there anything like Reality? Is it all Perception. Well it all depends on how they matter and to whom. Does Reality exist by itself? Is information and data useful if not processed in context to a framework? The same goes for Reality! Perceiving Reality on our own context sets up the world to be judged by us. Based on our assumptions and filters of our experiences. We have an image or perception or preconceived expectation of ourselves to begin with, others around us, how the world works and how it should. All this makes up for an interesting life executing our judgements and decisions on which we act.

Engaging the Energy of Life
https://youtu.be/4y35QrrO8qg
We drag ourselves around our lives with just about enough energy to reach the end of the day. How much are we paying Mindful attention to what our energy is creating or blocking? Developing energy that vibrates at higher frequencies creates positive attraction, attention, connection and influence. We create the energy field we operate within and connect with the world. And therefore we create the world we live in.

Connecting with Purpose Everyday
https://youtu.be/fU0I5YUo8hc
Everyday we are busy with the actions that make up life. Our goals and plans collide with the reality of each day. We strive, we cope, we do. Endlessly. But how much of it has meaning ? How does it connect with our purpose. The reason we live. The person we are. Who we want to truly be. Can everyday contribute in a small way to our future ? Can we get to that happy place where we know everyday that we have done something that is worthwhile and meaningful? Can we communicate that to ourselves to energize our lives, in place of the exhaustion and exasperation with our" human doing" rather than "human being" !

Leading Success with your Heart
https://youtu.be/TPadHbXiBt8
What's your Mantra for Success ? How do you balance Power, Success, Performance and People ? Merging the Mind with the Heart allows one to lead with Competence and also with Compassion, Courage and Character. It helps deliver outstanding results and create powerful relationships. Aligning Vision and Purpose with managing People, Performance and Practices. Coherence of Head, Heart and Hands.

The Sigma of Presentation Skills
https://youtu.be/Sl-EzwnHm6o
Make a great first impression ! But how?? !! Butterflies in the stomach, the mind blanking out, being transfixed or stuttering at the start could be your doom ! So use the SIGMA way to make a great start. One which will put you at ease and give you the confidence to make a great presentation. Of course there's a lot more to Presentation Design and Delivery. We shall keep that for another time !!

Communicating Assertively

LEADERSHIP IMPERATIVES

https://youtu.be/fWIKh-3eOH8
Our relationships influence the nature and quality of our communication. Assertiveness as a way of life is about being clear, firm and fair in communicating our intentions first and our behaviour based on securing an equitable result for everyone as much as possible. It's not possible to do this all the time, but if it is a large part of how we behave, people will ultimately respond in similar ways. Investing in relationships is a good way to call on them to address the needs of all people in the relationship. This does not mean that new or brief relationships need witness a free-for-all brawl or mute acceptance. It just means that when we practice assertiveness enough, it comes through in even the smaller moments of life. Our intentions get curated to a level at which even if communication breaks down, people feel safe enough to continue the conversation.

Live Life Beyond Learning & Assessments
https://youtu.be/jbi6CBI9K2E
Many among us would have received feedback on ourselves. As students our report cards served as feedback. As corporate citizens it's our performance assessment and conversations with our seniors. As adult learners we get various inputs from learning programs, learning models, audits and assessments - psychometric and others. Putting it all together can be quite a task. Perhaps we should just be listening in rather than being handcuffed to these. Filling in the blanks into our blindside can be useful. Does not mean we discard everything we know or think we know about ourselves. Rather we can use such inputs to also clarify, validate and curate the info we have. Remember that our lives are across a canvas far greater than the assessment windows and models which look at certain specific aspects of our lives in an interesting and insightful way. We are larger than the data. And the context within which we operate our lives is more dynamic. Let the context not suffer from the content. Yet let the content inform the context too!

Masks & Me

https://youtu.be/AogKMdbzAv8
Do you wear a mask? Yes we all do for different reasons. Most of them are to project an image. How authentic are we when for every good reason we project who we wish to be than who we really are? What is the benefit and how much does it cost us? How can we close the gap between the authentic self and the projected self? When can we evolve to authentically be the mask we wear?

Learn Life's Lessons Everyday
https://youtu.be/ptZP3zaMsCg
Everyday provides us moments of truth which indicate lessons we can use to make life better. Even the smallest lesson can turn to deliver the greatest benefit. How much are you paying attention to what your life and experiences are telling you?

Dance to Lifes' Music
https://youtu.be/HFZFB3HnO28
Everyday we live, we learn. Capture each lesson consciously. Share it with others. We live very different lives but surprisingly have very similar needs. The music of our lives can help other people dance through theirs !

Life is All Around You. Are you Present ?
https://youtu.be/LDuuuEClGd8
We hurry through life, trying to get to the other side. Success and Happiness. They are all somehow only in the Future. Can we notice the moment we are in ? What are we ignoring and perhaps losing in our race to the future ? When that too becomes the present, will we race through it too ? Arriving numbed and dazed at the end of life ?

LEADERSHIP IMPERATIVES

The Steering Wheel of Life-Edited
https://youtu.be/W0KdbtKwX6Q
Do you feel in control of life only when you are driving it? Are your hands locked on the steering wheel. Are you driving blind through traffic. Is there a chance you could fall asleep at the wheel? How do we deal with handing over the wheel to someone else? Is it always our car and our destination that matters? What do we need to consider on the shared journey of life such that we live as fully as possible in the moment whilst creating the future?

Steering Wheel & You !
https://youtu.be/yr4UTMy_UJ4
At the Steering Wheel of Life are you driving people Nuts??!! Is your focus so single minded that you drive by the moment and the magic of the process to a destination that denies you the journey itself? What does it mean to be obsessed with controlling the wheel of your life and all those in your car? At work how connected are you with your team? Are they empowered to drive your car? At home, are you so fixated at the wheel that it doesn't matter where others want to go, as long as they are going with you? How much will it take to unlock your grip from the wheel and embrace the journey together with others?

Driving Performance Excellence-Edited
https://youtu.be/FKHxgvzxWt8
Four Key Performance Drivers explained.

Our success lies in how we perform. How we perform lies in what drives us. What drives us depends on what motivates us and others. Motivation depends a lot on our emotional energy and our relationships with people we wish to impact with our performance ! We take a look at 4 Key Drivers : Communicating with Impact & Influence, Managing a Changing Environment, Performing through People with Empathy and Making a Personal Difference.

The Art of Winning Arguments
https://youtu.be/Z5xqVtBUNZc
Most of the time in the rush to decide things, our conversations, discussions and debates turn into Win-Lose Arguments. There are victors and there are the vanquished. Relationships fall apart. So perhaps we need to revisit the words we are using to describe these conversations in our minds. The way we position ourselves. The stances we adopt. The emotions were engage with. And the traffic jams of our collective egos we are stuck in.

Winning "Arguments" without Losing Relationships. Needs you to Change your Language, Reframe Communication, Take Responsibility, Enlist support, Engage Empathy and convert arguments into productive high energy courageous conversations.

Asserting your EQ
https://youtu.be/LHwsTi9p0Q0

Assertiveness is the key to EQ. Communicating is crucial to managing Relationships and Results. Communicating with Emotional Balance is how we demonstrate emotional intelligence. Powerful, trustworthy, authentic and reliable relationships help us get to the results we desire. Assertiveness is a critical milestone on pathway to an EQ life!

The Code of the Road
https://youtu.be/pPvjbB_A7zk

The roads we travel on and the traffic we negotiate everyday are uncannily like life itself. Here we take a look at what quick lessons we can learn on the roads of life and put them to work in life itself.

LEADERSHIP IMPERATIVES

Music credit : Dreamy Dreamers by Samsung Galaxy A50s mobile phone video editing software

Claim your Rightful Life
https://youtu.be/1TlBeKJloml

Little things do matter. The permissions you give define the quality of your life. Announce your Life is about claiming your right to a life that is fair, just, equitable and civil. It's about setting your boundaries. We teach others how to treat us by the way we treat ourselves. We need to stand up, smile and say something! Because it matters !!

Who are you ?
https://youtu.be/i1MdAlr9Alc

We often define our lives by what we do. Yet we are not truly products of our profession or qualifications or achievements. That's why some people great success stories are riddled with doubt and unhappy with their lives. Finding out the answer to Who You Are can help find Purpose and redefine your life. Or of course endorse your life. Either way, it's good to answer the question Who Are You !

Engaging EQ Energy
https://youtu.be/b9M-VapoAN4

This is the first Episode in the series Engaging EQ Energy. It's about understanding Emotional Intelligence, the role of emotions themselves, the EQ Framework and How one can engage the 3 Pursuits of the EQ Competences as defined by Six Seconds, California, USA, world leaders in the study and application of EQ.
LESSONS FROM THE CROSS OF CRISIS
https://youtu.be/wXLvfAi5mxl

Every crisis has several lessons to learn from. Currently the world is plunged into the chaos of the Coronavirus Crisis. Our very existence is threatened. Panic has taken over the reins of what we once knew to be a regulated, planned and organized life. Pressing the Pause Button has put the world face to face with the most dreadful reality of our times. Yet there are compelling lessons to learn as we survive this gut wrenching turbulence. Five Lessons emerge with practical wisdom which we can harness to negotiate our passage through life.

Making Relationships Count
https://youtu.be/qlKMHckXWW0

We are often held hostage by our friendships and relationships. Burdened by the responsibility of managing the imbalances and inequities of the relationship. Taking the blame in order to keep the peace. An unfair friendship is destructive. Manipulative relationships make doormats of people who are unwilling to call out the unfairness and have conversations about how it needs to be. Beware of being a victim or victimizing others in friendships where too much is being asked of the other almost all of the time.

Fingerprinting Success
https://youtu.be/QCucf5n-1G0

Just as our fingerprint is an unique identification of each of us as individuals, success too has an unique DNA or Fingerprint of how we engage our Values, our Goals and our Emotions which hold them together and give them life and direction. It's all in our hands, literally and figuratively!! Here we look at an interesting way to count our Values and Goals on our fingers and look at what we hold in the palms of our hands. Our Core Values and Our Vision which together script the Legacy of our Lives

LEADERSHIP IMPERATIVES

REWIRING Life Beyond COVID-19
https://youtu.be/co_uA-fZoGA

The world is under siege and we are besieged with the fear of the unknown and unseen. Never before have we had to change the context of our lives so dramatically. We can take this time and opportunity to rewire and reimagine our lives beyond the uncertainty and disruption we are struggling to live through.

To REFRAME our lives is to recreate the context within which we operate, moving from Panic & Paralysis to Productivity.

R : Review & Reflect on what are thoughts are in the moment
E : Engagement Levels of our Emotions and Actions
F : Focus on FIVE important issues
R : Draw up a Rewiring Plan.
A : Activate the Plan
M : Measure Progress, Mend the Plan to work better
E : Educate, Enlarge & Energize your Reframed life

Locked Down & Locked Into Life
https://youtu.be/GIqaSCqqw4w

Learning to deal with the lockdown allows us to revisit our lives. And learn as students of the game, once again. Stay Home Stay Safe and Stay a Student of Life. This is Life sending us Back to School !

Living a Re-Loaded Life !
https://youtu.be/0VuMZWsGIps

The old ways die away as we learn to cope in the new world of 2020. This is a year we shall never forget. Stories shall be told of how we fought the Coronavirus and survived How the world stopped its mad dash to an insane future. How we recreated or were forced to recreate the world which we had dismantled and almost destroyed. Let's make sure we are part of that story. Let's give ourselves reasons to succeed Time to think how we need to revitalize old ways, values and behaviour to succeed in the new context that this scourge has thrown to recast the very vitality of life

Lockdown into your Legacy_ Rewrite your Story
https://youtu.be/7NZ_KXPEPPk

Use the coronavirus lockdown to look into rewriting the story of your life. Thread the significant moments of your life and see how your story had developed and defined life. Most of us have lived significant lives in many ways. Let's take that forward and leave a legacy. Something that lives beyond us as a gift to those who follow. This year 2020 is a landmark year in human history. Let it scare us to survive and thrive with renewed vigour and vitality. Let new powerful stories emerge beyond the lockdown ! Unlock the amazing stories from rest of your life !

The Power of Your Life Story !
https://youtu.be/n-54JHAgrF0

Our life is on Pause. It is the perfect gift of time and opportunity to look into rewriting the story of your life. Stitch the significant moments of your life driven by powerful emotions and see how your story had developed and defined life. What is the DNA of your life ? How is it going to help you ? This year 2020 is a landmark year in human history. Let new powerful stories emerge beyond the lockdown ! Emerge from the shadows to the light of the life of the future you are scripting today.

You can contact Dexter Valles here

DEXTER JOHN VALLES
CEO & Managing Consultant, Valmar International
Founder Director, The EQ Legion of India

Facebook https://www.facebook.com/dexvalles
LinkedIn https://www.linkedin.com/in/dextervalles
Twitter @dynamodex
Website 1 http://www.valmarinternational.com
Website 2
https://dextervalles.wixsite.com/website
Email : dexter@valmarinternational.com

Credits and References

All elements of this book are the original creative work of the author Dexter John Valles

Chapter Nine : The EQ Savvy Leader : Heart Centered Leadership has been adapted from my book @The Steering Wheel of Life : Success Scripts. EQ Competencies referred to can be learned in greater detail from Six Seconds www.6seconds.org (also see below)

Reading Reference

Emotional Intelligence

Six Seconds www.6seconds.org World Leaders in EQ (the largest EQ Network in the World)

Economic Crisis of 2020

https://www.worldbank.org/en/news/feature/2020/06/08/the-global-economic-outlook-during-the-covid-19-pandemic-a-changed-world

https://www.weforum.org/agenda/2019/12/global-trade-wto-china-us-america/

Digital Leadership and Artificial Intelligence

www.cmswire.com/digital-workplace/8-skills-every-digital-leader-needs/

https://elmosoftware.com.au/resources/blog/leadership-disrupted-how-to-be-a-digital-leader/

https://www.zdnet.com/article/what-is-ai-everything-you-need-to-know-about-artificial-intelligence/

LEADERSHIP IMPERATIVES

OTHER BOOKS BY THIS AUTHOR

INSPIRED BY THE HOLY SPIRIT

Available on www.amazon.com in Kindle and Paperback

Living & Leading Beyond 2020

The Butterfly Blueprint

Managing Transformative Change

Dexter Valles

THE BUTTERFLY BLUEPRINT
Managing Transformative Change

Metamorphosis is an incredibly fascinating journey of transitioning the ordinary caterpillar to a magnificent butterfly! It needs patience and care. Just as our own life must go through metamorphosis from helplessness to strength, from being unskilled and inept to being skilled and agile! Yet in our impatience we often wake up the Caterpillar in ourselves and others too, halfway through the metamorphosis, hoping that the butterfly within has already formed

Even before any of the magic has been displayed, we want this butterfly to grow its wings and fly. Our competitive speeding world in which we live today, brings us breathlessly close to the threshold of destroying the cocoon and the magical metamorphosis within it. The cocoon after all, is that fragile vehicle and the extraordinarily painstaking process which transforms the Ugly Caterpillar into the Beautiful Butterfly.

Every caterpillar must bide its' time to be born a butterfly. The butterfly too, must be released from the memories of the cocoon, to fly gracefully in fields of flowers. The lessons from the cocoon are now invisible part of butterfly beauty and grace. That's the Butterfly Blueprint ! The Cocoon meets the Sky !

We take a look at what it means to design, engage and coach the Butterfly Blueprint. This book deals with this journey in Four Parts. Beginning with the Caterpillar, it's Metamorphosis, and finally the Butterfly ! We also look at the role of emotions accompanying the journey of the Butterfly Blueprint. To converge the Blueprint to everyday actions and advice, we Engage the Blueprint into FIVE Focus Areas in the Butterfly Blueprint's Flight

LEADERSHIP IMPERATIVES

@ THE STEERING WHEEL OF LIFE
Success Scripts

This book has several Success Scripts on various aspects of life Each article has its very own precious nugget of wisdom. Beginning with ASPIRE for Success, the book leads you through a gallery of rich portraits of life like Leading on the Edge, Eek-onomics - Managing in Tough Times, Leading & Engaging Emotional Energy – Emotional Intelligence practical wisdom and practices, an interestingly christened article The Street Clothes of Respect, Relating with Emotional Purpose which looks at crafting Successful Relationships and several more gems to add sparkle and paint to the portrait of a successful life.

These Success Scripts have been compiled to offer the reader an opportunity to design a Personal Success Script after learning from the insights in each article.

No Success Script is final and absolute. Each one must write and rewrite their scripts to meet the changing times and life experiences while steering the ship of their lives across the seas and oceans of change.

It is a compilation of such wisdom-pods which can appeal and relate to different people for different reasons. And to you too, at different points of your life.

You must ultimately write your own success script. That's when you shall take charge of the wheel and steer the ship of your life to the wide-open seas of success.

Living & Leading Beyond 2020

LEADERSHIP IMPERATIVES

THE CODE OF THE ROAD
Navigating Life's Traffic Lanes

This book is a product of my everyday life, driving around in the heavily congested roads of my beloved city Mumbai in INDIA

I would end my day feeling an overwhelming rush of mixed emotions and found it really hard to shrug off the strong connections to everyday Life ! As I reflected on what I could learn from these experiences, interesting relationships began to form and make strange sense to me.

All travelers have encountered Roadblocks along their journeys. The 5 Road Block Lessons offer interesting insight into the usefulness of Roadblocks on the Road of Life. Navigating Life's Traffic Lanes takes you through 12 Lane Laws of Life each translated into a cryptic Life Lesson.

The Road of Life as you shall discover, is governed by The Code of the Road. The book takes you on a road trip through three segments – Your Car, The Road and The Code putting it all together in a delightful summary called You, The Road and the Code. Enjoy the Ride !

CONNECTED TO SOUL

Igniting Human Spirit with Purpose

This book explores the essence of life and the human spirit connected to the soul. That eternal part of us which ignites our purpose and passion. This creates meaning drawn from what we do and allows us leave a Legacy. This Legacy rides forward on that fuel of Purpose with Passion long after we have stopped stoking the fire ourselves.

Man is eternally in search of two major engines to drive life. The Engines of Purpose and Provision. These create direction and meaning. The truth is that one does not often find both together. Yet either one has the power to deeply engage the human spirit.

Engaging Energy or Passion would depend on where the engagement lies. Together these engines enable us engage the incredible and enormous power of an ignited life!

The journey of this book winds across 3 Parts. Each Part has 4 Ways of looking at the theme of that part. The chapters in each part describe their story of this book in their own unique ways. As if each chapter is written from a different view of life. In a way, as a reader you get 12 different views of the book, almost just like life is most of the time. Together they bring to the reader, the essence of the entire story of the book itself.

Living & Leading Beyond 2020

FLAWED yet PRECIOUS

Leading a Sparkling Life

As time flows by, we often look back at all the years gone by, and strive to understand what life has taught us. What can we do better? What would really need to be New in the coming Year?? What needs to change?

I feel it's more about incremental steps of self-revelation. Peeling off the onion rings. Increasing vulnerability. In the place of numbness. I realize that as long as we find our way to live with integrity, strip the deceit and strive for authenticity in our lives , be mindful of our behaviour as we relate with others, and develop deeper consciousness of who we are in each moment; we can evolve to be the person in every essence we truly are and meant to be.

We can then relate to others in ways that release them to be and live the luminous lives they too are.

While this may seem complex in the way we practice living, tiptoeing around our realities, adding layers of interpretations to what's in plain sight, in truth, the simpler we make our everyday explanations the easier they are to access and engage across the experiences we create for ourselves and others. And here's the shocker. We can guarantee mistakes!! But you see, that's how we are too... Flawed yet precious. Flawed in our human-ness, Precious in the divinity of our dreams and aspirations nurtured within

THE WARRIOR LEADER

INSPIRE. INFLUENCE. IGNITE

Dexter Valles

LEADERSHIP IMPERATIVES

THE WARRIOR LEADER
INSPIRE.INFLUENCE.IGNITE

This book looks at life through the eyes of leadership. A leadership with a special style. Not just to lead with, but to live with. This is the Warrior Leader. Fierce. Focused. Courageous. Competent. Compassionate. And importantly, Visionary. Versatile. Resilient. Ignited. Agile.

A Lethal array of Arrows in the Warrior Leader's Quiver. To pierce through the darkness and storm of turbulence, chaos and disruption. To reach the distant verdant hills of a flourishing life-scape which hold the heart of hope that yearns to beat once again in the bosom of humanity.

The Warrior Leader is an absorbing tale of Strong Goal Oriented Leadership, leveraging Four Attributes : Visionary, Versatile, Resilient, and Lethal

These Four Attributes are innate to a Warrior Leader. Almost like the DNA Genetic Code of such leaders. They often operate unconsciously from these when faced with crisis or crisis like circumstances. You can sense the energy radiate around a Warrior Leader and will find yourself bathed in that aura. Nothing seems too difficult or desperate when a Warrior Leader leads the way.

It's now time to realize that that very magic lies within each one of us. The Warrior Leader lives in each one of us. This book helps you create your very own Agile Warrior Leader's Battlefield Blueprint.

5 FLAGS OF LIFE
The Essence of Living & Leading Today

The Flag is probably the oldest symbol of identity, representation, honour, pride, presence and conquest. It has been used for various reasons ever since the time it was first raised as a military symbol and as a representation of national identity.

The Flag has been used to communicate both the tangible and intangible in everyday conversation. You would have used it often enough yourself. To Unfurl the Flag as a symbol of pride, hope and unique identity, to Plant the Flag in conquest, to Fly the Flag in defiance, bravado, mastery or even to surrender, to Raise the Flag on issues, to Flag Off a race, to Salute the Flag with Respect, to Keep the Flag Flying in continuous mastery and dominance.

The 5 Flags of Life are each of these and all of these. Each Flag is a symbol of your growing identity, prowess, pride, hope, dominance, mastery, conquest, respect.

Plant, Raise, Unfurl, Fly and Salute each Flag to create your unique identity and presence in life.

And finally, design your very own flag ! One which emblazons your identity with pride, for the world to recognize and acknowledge.

www.ingramcontent.com/pod-product-compliance
Lightning Source LLC
Chambersburg PA
CBHW071406210526
45465CB00001B/276